S. HRG. 107–889

HOMELAND SECURITY: ASSESSING THE NEEDS OF LOCAL LAW ENFORCEMENT

HEARING

BEFORE THE

SUBCOMMITTEE ON CRIME AND DRUGS

OF THE

COMMITTEE ON THE JUDICIARY UNITED STATES SENATE

ONE HUNDRED SEVENTH CONGRESS

SECOND SESSION

MARCH 21, 2002

Serial No. J–107–70

Printed for the use of the Committee on the Judiciary

U.S. GOVERNMENT PRINTING OFFICE

85–884 PDF WASHINGTON : 2003

For sale by the Superintendent of Documents, U.S. Government Printing Office
Internet: bookstore.gpo.gov Phone: toll free (866) 512–1800; DC area (202) 512–1800
Fax: (202) 512–2250 Mail: Stop SSOP, Washington, DC 20402–0001

COMMITTEE ON THE JUDICIARY

PATRICK J. LEAHY, Vermont, *Chairman*

EDWARD M. KENNEDY, Massachusetts	ORRIN G. HATCH, Utah
JOSEPH R. BIDEN, JR., Delaware	STROM THURMOND, South Carolina
HERBERT KOHL, Wisconsin	CHARLES E. GRASSLEY, Iowa
DIANNE FEINSTEIN, California	ARLEN SPECTER, Pennsylvania
RUSSELL D. FEINGOLD, Wisconsin	JON KYL, Arizona
CHARLES E. SCHUMER, New York	MIKE DEWINE, Ohio
RICHARD J. DURBIN, Illinois	JEFF SESSIONS, Alabama
MARIA CANTWELL, Washington	SAM BROWNBACK, Kansas
JOHN EDWARDS, North Carolina	MITCH MCCONNELL, Kentucky

BRUCE A. COHEN, *Majority Chief Counsel and Staff Director*
SHARON PROST, *Minority Chief Counsel*
MAKAN DELRAHIM, *Minority Staff Director*

SUBCOMMITTEE ON CRIME AND DRUGS

JOSEPH R. BIDEN, JR., Delaware, *Chairman*

PATRICK J. LEAHY, Vermont	CHARLES E. GRASSLEY, Iowa
DIANNE FEINSTEIN, California	ORRIN G. HATCH, Utah
HERBERT KOHL, Wisconsin	MIKE DEWINE, Ohio
RICHARD J. DURBIN, Illinois	JEFF SESSIONS, Alabama
MARIA CANTWELL, Washington	SAM BROWNBACK, Kansas
JOHN EDWARDS, North Carolina	MITCH MCCONNELL, Kentucky

GEORGE ELLARD, *Majority Chief Counsel*
RITA LARI, *Minority Chief Counsel*

CONTENTS

STATEMENTS OF COMMITTEE MEMBERS

WITNESSES

SUBMISSIONS FOR THE RECORD

HOMELAND SECURITY: ASSESSING THE NEEDS OF LOCAL LAW ENFORCEMENT

THURSDAY, MARCH 21, 2002

U.S. SENATE,
SUBCOMMITTEE ON CRIME AND DRUGS,
COMMITTEE ON THE JUDICIARY,
Washington, DC.

The subcommittee met, pursuant to notice, at 2:07 p.m., in room SD–226, Dirksen Senate Office Building, Hon. Joseph R. Biden, Jr., (chairman of the subcommittee) presiding.

STATEMENT OF HON. JOSEPH R. BIDEN, JR., A U.S. SENATOR FROM THE STATE OF DELAWARE

Chairman BIDEN. The subcommittee will come to order, please. I welcome all our witnesses today and will explain what all of them know, because it is not the first time some have been here.

As the subcommittee opens this hearing, our Subcommittee on Crime and Drugs, there is a lot unfortunately going on today, so some of my colleagues will be in and out.

Mayor Hood, of Orlando, is going to be here. She is necessarily delayed for a few minutes, and I have sought and gained the permission through her staff to be able to begin in her absence. She was going to be our lead-off witness.

Senator Grassley will be here. Senator Grassley has taken an inordinately strong interest in the subject before us. And it is funny, but the more things change, the more they remain the same. Twenty-eight years ago, I started off as chairman of this subcommittee and now I am chairman of this subcommittee again. So it just goes to show that I think it is vitally important, the subject we are going to be dealing with today.

I have an opening statement, and hopefully Senator Grassley may be here by then and he will make an opening statement. Then we will turn to our witnesses and I will announce the order after I introduce each of you. Again, thank you all for being here.

I called this hearing this afternoon because I wanted to hear from the mayors and the men and women in local law enforcement, as well as some scholars who have very decided views on the President's proposed budget for fiscal year 2003. First, let me point out a few things.

Over the past 8 years, spending on local law enforcement has funded close to an additional 114,000 new officers on our streets. Now, let me be precise, lest someone immediately corrects me. There are probably somewhat in excess—I don't know the exact numbers on the chart, but we have roughly 83,000 new shields; that is, we are hiring 83,000 new police officers who have a shield.

The remainder of that comes from what we call the COPS MORE program, allowing mayors and others to go out and hire other people to allow a shield, a badge, a sworn police officer to be out on the street. The way it has been calculated by the COPS Office and by the last two administrations, roughly 114,000 more officers are on the street and involved in community policing than were at the start of this whole process.

Over the same period, as you can see from the graph, crime has dropped 28 percent overall. Now, again, I know people say because I drafted the COPS legislation and what was originally called the Biden crime bill—actually, it was originally the Biden-Hatch crime bill, until it got to the House of Representatives, and then all of a sudden my friends on this side of the aisle, the Republicans, didn't like it anymore and it became the Biden crime bill, although we did get seven Republicans to vote for it back in 1994.

Then President Clinton thought, and I agreed with him, that it should be the Clinton crime bill. Then the Democrats lost the election in 1994 and he started calling it the Biden crime bill again, and then when he found out how popular it was it became the Clinton crime bill. I think Chief Szczerba can tell you the only place where it has always been called the Biden crime bill is Delaware.

But it doesn't matter whose crime bill it is. The reason I mention it is this: I do have a keen interest, in that I, along with police officers, beginning in 1990 wrote this bill. But I want to say up front up here I do not claim that it is totally responsible for that reduction in crime. I don't believe we could have seen the reduction in crime we have seen were it not for the crime bill, but I do not suggest that is the only reason why crime came down.

So I don't want to get us into an internecine debate about whether or not COPS is totally responsible for all the decrease in crime, but there are two things that are clear. One, there have been authorized 114,000 more police officers to walk the street than were walking the street in 1993 locally. Second, crime has dropped 28 percent.

The drop in the rates of victimization, or what most people think of as violent crime or crimes against individuals, has been even more dramatic. From 1994, the year of the passage of the crime bill, to the year 2000, the rate of victimization of violent crime—that is, rape, robbery, assault, and homicide—has dropped a total of 46 percent.

In 1994, if I had said to anybody when we passed that crime bill when I was arguing for its passage on the floor—if I had said if you vote for this crime bill, crime is going to drop by overall 28 percent and violent crime by 46 percent, I would have thought I was certifiable, and I am sure Charlton Heston would have had something to say about it. He is the guy who called this the welfare bill for social workers.

The truth of the matter is it has been astounding, which I would note parenthetically goes to show you what you can do when you empower people to make their own decisions and let local governments and the people who know what they are doing actually apply for this money and actually decide how they want to use it.

In 1994, we made a decision that the Federal Government ought to be in the business of encouraging police departments to act and to move into the community policing business. We decided then that we ought to help police departments get their officers out from behind their desks and out of their cars and onto the streets.

The crime bill kind of reminds me of Social Security. The overhead is incredibly low, the success is very high, and we take it for granted. So what is the big deal? I want to remind everybody that when we decided to provide—and only one part of the crime was COPS; there were three parts. One was prisons, out of a $30 billion bill, and the other part was prevention and treatment, prevention primarily.

What we intended to do was to quite frankly figure out, Mr. Mayor, how we could leverage you all into doing what was difficult to do. Back then, Chief Szczerba was on patrol, probably, but the truth of the matter is cops didn't want to be involved in community policing. The reason they didn't is it is a heck of a lot harder. It takes more manpower, it takes more resources, it is more difficult.

So remember the deal here. The deal was in the original COPS bill that in order to get any money to hire a new shield—if you had a department of 100 people, to get one federally funded cop, you had to put all 101 on the street. You had to commit all 101 to community policing. You couldn't get one if your department didn't move to community policing. Number two, if you had 100 cops that you hired then and your end strength was 100, you couldn't fire one or let one go and add a federally-funded cop. You would get no money.

I got here in 1972 as a 29-year-old kid. I was elected to the United States Senate, and I had been a local official and I used to go through all those hearings in the country council when the county executive would say or the president of the counsel would say we are going to do such-and-such. And I would say, well, how much would that cost? And they would say it is not going to cost anything; that is Federal money. I know local officials say they don't say that, but sometimes they do. That is Federal money.

I remember we had a program called LEAA, the Law Enforcement Assistance Administration. The first thing I did got me in trouble. The chairman of the subcommittee I now am chairing was a fellow named McClellan, from Arkansas, one of the most powerful, toughest guys in the Senate and a fellow Democrat. He was the author of the LEAA program and the first major move I made was to eliminate the LEAA program, and oh, my Lord, did I hear about that.

But the reason I did it was in the city of Wilmington, as Chief Szczerba may remember, the city was, for example, laying off policemen and laying off fireman and hiring them back with Federal money. The end result was not one additional cop and not one additional fireman at the end of the day. County officials would say, look, we didn't raise your taxes, but we kept the end strength of the police department up.

So the point to remember here is in the program that has functioned up to now, the one being eliminated, you had to keep the end strength of your department up. If you are authorized at 100, you had better have 100. If you go down to 90, you don't get any

Federal money. If you are 5,000 and you go down to 4,999, you don't get any Federal money. That was, if you will, the stick that went along with the carrot, and you all did incredibly well.

Today, over 7 years after passage of the crime bill, the COPS program has awarded $7.4 billion over the period to authorize 113,900 new officers, 83,000 of whom are on the streets today. The reason I say on the streets today is some are still being trained. The departments got the money; the cities, the counties, the States and the towns got the money and their officer that they hired is literally going through the police academy now. They are not all on the street yet.

Now, 86 percent of all law enforcement agencies in the United States of America, every single police department, from a 2-person police department in a small town to a city with many thousands of police as New York has—86 percent of all the police departments in America are engaged in what we call community policing. The number of community police officers increased by 4,055 from 1997 to 1999 alone. Last December, this subcommittee held a hearing to highlight a new study indicating that the COPS grants had indeed reduced crime. These graphs make the point.

So where do we go from here? The administration has put forward its vision, a big increase for first responders, increases which are needed and quite frankly which I support. I introduced a bill 18 months ago, before 9/11, calling for $1 billion being made available to firefighters for training, local firefighters, for training and support.

I have concerns, however, about whether the panel assembled here will actually see any of the money. Now, two of the panelists are not going to see any money. If they did, they would be put in jail because they are from think tanks, but the truth of the matter is I am referring to the mayors and the local officials.

I am worried that FEMA, which is a fine, fine agency, may not be the right agency to fund these homeland security needs. But at the same time the administration boasts spending much more money for homeland defense—and they should; it is a significant increase—they have made huge cuts in local law enforcement programs. They cut two areas that I want to highlight this afternoon.

Overall, the administration has slashed funds to the men and women of law enforcement by about 36 percent from last year. First, they want to end the COPS program totally. No dollars are included for any new hiring, no dollars are included for school resource officers, and the COPS technology program is cut by two-thirds.

Now, for those in the audience who don't know what the COPS technology program is, that is allowing police officers to have, for example, laptops in their cars. One of the things that the chiefs and NAPO and FOP and others have taught me over the years is when a cop has to go back after making an arrest, minor or major, to the station house to bang out the report, it takes time, it takes effort. It is clerical, it is necessary, it is important, but no one is on the street.

If that police officer can pull over to the side of the road and take out a laptop computer and bang in what he or she needs to bang in for that report, the cop is still on the street, still available on call, and it takes a lot less time. So those are the kinds of things we have used these technology programs for, and they cut that by two-thirds.

Enactment of this budget would mean that we cannot put an additional 4,500 new officers on the streets of America next year. We could not put more than 1,600 more resource officers into schools around the country.

Now, I want to tell you, in my State—and I don't know about Arkansas; I suspect it is the same, Mr. Mayor—these school resource officers have been a phenomenal hit, like everything else that COPS has done. They have had a synergistic impact on things. It wasn't only that they were in a school, in uniform, at a particular high school or school to keep the peace. What they found is they built relationships with individual students and they built relationships with the community.

Now, the kid who wouldn't trust anybody to go up and say, you know, Johnny brought a gun to school, or I heard Billy and Molly talking about how they are going to take out the cafeteria, or by the way I think there is a drug deal going down in the gym, they now know there is someone they can trust. They have actually built relationships.

I think you are going to see—we have not done them yet—serious studies done showing that where there is a police resource officer in a public school, you have seen that it has an incredible impact not only in increasing the safety in the school, but also impacting upon the kinds of transgressions that occur within those schools. Eliminating a program like this which has been critically important to the crime drop, I think, would be penny-wise and pound-foolish. Frankly, I agree with the Attorney General, who testified not too long ago, when he said that the COPS program has been a miraculous success.

Madam Mayor, welcome. It is great to have you. We have a seat right up front for you. We wouldn't dare start without you. All these guys said they were not going to go until you came. Welcome. I appreciate your making the effort.

The second point I want to make is that the administration merges a time-honored and tested program, the so-called Byrne grants, with the Local Law Enforcement Block Grant program, one that was quite frankly more the brain child of my Republican colleagues which I supported that worked very, very well.

Merging these two things sounds okay until you learn that when you merge them, you end up with 20 percent fewer funds than you had when they were separate. It reminds me of that old game on the boardwalk where the guy has three shells and one pea and he moves them all around. Well, the difference in this game is there is no pea under the shell. I mean, you combine the two and you get 20 percent less money in the name of efficiency, and that is represented on the graph we have up here now.

That would mean fewer crime prevention programs, fewer drug courts, which I know in Florida have been an incredible success—quite frankly, we modeled the national program after Florida—fewer jail cells, and fewer treatment programs in each of your localities. Mayors and police chiefs around the country are concerned about these proposals, based on the inquiries I have received, and they are facing budget freezes at the same time.

By the way, let me make it clear I don't have a single doubt that the President of the United States, the Attorney General and the entire administration are as opposed to crime and are as dedicated to eliminating crime as any administration in the history of the United States of America. I don't have any doubt about that. I don't have any doubt about them being tough on crime.

What I am arguing with is their tactics. What I am arguing with is their strategy on how to deal with crime, and they are radically changing the strategy here, the strategy that has worked pretty well for the last eight years.

So at the very time we are changing this strategy, three other phenomena are occurring. Every governor in the country is in some kind of trouble now economically, not because they are not good governors. They are fine governors, but the national economy has taken a real hit. 9/11 has put a real hit on the economy, and other things I won't mention because we may disagree on why. But the bottom line is, although there are some recovery signs that we are coming out of this recession, State budgets are being significantly trimmed. My own State is a case in point. City budgets and city revenues are down. Business is down, business revenues are down, and cities have much more difficulty finding tax bases and resources than even States do.

The second factor that has occurred at the same time we are making these kinds of cuts is that the FBI, which is overwhelmed—if they haven't already come to you, Chief Szczerba or Mayor Hood, or others, they are going to be coming to you saying, guess what, we can't do all we did in your city before; bank robberies aren't going to be on our watch anymore; interstate car thefts are going to have to be a local problem.

Now, depending on the jurisdiction, the FBI co-jurisdiction—and we have been happy to let them exercise it—that jurisdiction has ranged from representing anywhere from 5 to 20 percent of the law enforcement needs in some communities. The FBI is not going to be doing that anymore.

The last thing—and I need not tell a mayor the size of the city of Orlando, but every time we necessarily go on alert as a Nation, if she doesn't keep her cops' overtime, if she doesn't make sure everybody is standing ready in the airport at Orlando, which is as big as my State just about—I mean, think about this. Think about the additional strain on the budgets of the mayors, the governors, and the county executives when we go to that red color; we didn't have it before, but when we go to high alert that there may be an attack. That has been an incredible strain on your budgets.

So all of this is being telescoped into one moment here and my concern is not only are we not going to fund more cops, but I think you are going to have great difficulty in the cities and States maintaining the number of cops you now have over the next couple of years. I hope I am wrong about that, I hope I am wrong.

The Conference of Mayors and the League of Cities, made up of local elected officials from both parties, contacted me last month to voice their concerns. That is why I scheduled this hearing today so the Senate could hear from them directly. So let's have a discussion today about programs that are important to the mayors and the chiefs.

How has the COPS program been helpful to you, if it has? How does it fit into your new homeland security mission? What will its elimination mean for public safety in the future? How have the Byrne grants and local law enforcement block grants been used? Have they been effective? Should they be merged, should they change? Most importantly, what do you need from us so that you can keep the crime rates down and meet your new homeland security responsibilities at the same time?

As I am sure some of the panel are tired of hearing me say, crime is like cutting grass; it is like cutting grass. I can cut my grass the first good growth it gets and my lawn will look perfect. If I don't cut it for another three weeks, it is going to look like hell. The grass grows.

The idea that we can keep crime rates down as we have and keep them at these lower levels or reduce them further by spending less money, having fewer cops, having less input, I would respectfully suggest to you is like you cutting your lawn the first day of summer and putting your lawn mower away for the rest of the summer. The weeds will grow back and you are going to have a forest on your front lawn. That is what is going to happen, in my view, if we do not adequately fund law enforcement.

With that, let me suggest that we move to our witness list. We have a very distinguished panel with us this afternoon. First, we will hear from the Mayor of North Little Rock, Arkansas, Patrick Henry Hays. He has seen the whites of their eyes and he has arrested them. Mayor Hays is here on behalf of the U.S. Conference of Mayors. He practiced law in North Little Rock from 1973 to 1988, when he was elected to his first four-year term as mayor. Mayor Hays is now serving his fourth term. As my mother Jean Finnegan Biden would say, no purgatory for him, straight to heaven. Four terms as mayor is beyond my capacity.

Next, we will hear from the past president of the National League of Cities, Mayor Glenda Hood, of Orlando, Florida. Mayor Hood has been a leader among the mayors and she has served as mayor since 1992. Before that, she was a member of the Orlando City Council and was president of her own public relations firm. Mayor Hood is an Orlando native and a fourth-generation Floridian, which means that she is probably Seminole. I didn't know anybody was around for four generations. It is good to see you again, Mayor Hood, and we truly welcome you here.

Next, we will hear from Chief Michael Szczerba, of the Wilmington Police Department. Chief Szczerba has served in the Patrol Division, the Drug and Organized Crime Divisions, the Community Service Division, and now as chief of our police. He is a lifelong resident of Wilmington. He is a graduate of the high school that was the chief competitor of the Catholic high school I went to—that is the only reason I didn't like him at first—I am only joking; that is a joke, Chief—and the University of Delaware, my alma mater. Thanks for coming down this afternoon.

Also on the panel this afternoon will be Bill Johnson, Executive Director of the National Association of Police Organizations, NAPO, which I would credit more than any other outfit for the crime bill being passed in the first place, particularly Mr. Scully, who was your predecessor. They were instrumental in passing the bill in 1994.

Bill, I am glad to have you here today.

Bill Johnson is a former police officer and prosecutor. He served with the old Orchard Branch, Maine, Police Department, and then with the Miami, Florida, State's attorney's office. Bill is a native of Chicago. He received his undergraduate degree from Brown University and his law degree from Georgetown.

I would like to welcome you, Bill.

Tommy Ferrell is the sheriff of Adams County, Mississippi. Where I come from, notwithstanding the chief, I like the sheriffs on my side. The sheriff is the First Vice President of the National Sheriffs' Association.

People who come from States where they don't rely on sheriffs as much should understand that they are a significant law enforcement element. In many cases, they control the prisons in their counties, as well as they do law enforcement duties.

He will soon be sworn in as president of that organization later this year. Chief Ferrell began his law enforcement career in 1969 and is presently in his third term as sheriff. He also serves as a lieutenant colonel in the military police branch of the Army National Guard.

Thank you for being here, Sheriff.

Finally, David Muhlhausen is a policy analyst, and a really first-rate one, from the Heritage Foundation. He holds a master's degree in policy sciences from the University of Maryland. This is his second appearance before this subcommittee and I thank him for coming back. We learned a lot from his first appearance.

So, Mayor Hays, if you will, will you please proceed?

STATEMENT OF HON. PATRICK HENRY HAYS, MAYOR, LITTLE ROCK, AR, ON BEHALF OF THE U.S. CONFERENCE OF MAYORS

Mayor HAYS. Senator, it is good to be with you again, and I might add you began my career in 1973. Actually, in 1971 I had a chance to come up here from Arkansas and work on the staff of John McClellan. I came back in 1972 and was in the Office of General Counsel for LEAA for a summer, and had an opportunity to do a little bit of legal work. I think that agency had run its course and I think the movement toward its elimination was a wise act by Congress.

Also, what we are doing here now in regard to the continuation of the COPS program is extremely important, and I want to thank you for calling today's hearing, as well as Senator Grassley and the entire subcommittee.

Mayors have consistently attached a high priority to preparing our cities for the possibility of disasters, both natural and man-made. Now, in the wake of September 11 and the anthrax mailings, emergency management planning has been redoubled and there have been significant new deployments of public safety resources.

The Conference of Mayors released a survey which found that from September 11, 2001, to the end of 2002, cities will spend an additional $2.6 billion on new homeland security priorities, including equipment, overtime, and training.

I might add, Senator, it seems like you have been in city halls around the country because of your opening statement reflects a lot of what I am going to mirror in my comments.

Mayors know the importance of public safety and are one hundred percent committed to the homeland war against terrorism, but we must forge a new Federal-local partnership to make sure that our domestic soldiers—police, fire and emergency workers, and other city employees—have the resources to meet this new challenge. This was the message that mayors and police chiefs carried to Congress last week, and I again wanted to thank you for participating in our discussions and that press conference that was held out in front of the Capitol.

In October of 2001, the Conference of Mayors sponsored a safety and security summit, at which we developed a national action plan covering transportation security, emergency management, and law enforcement.

I might ask the Senator if we could enter this into the record of these proceedings.

Chairman BIDEN. Yes, both will be entered into the record, if that is all right.

Mayor HAYS. That would be my hope. Thank you, Senator.

Regarding supporting our first responders, Senator, if I could add, at our January 24 White House meeting this year, with over 300 mayors present, President Bush announced his $3.5 billion first responders initiative, which we praised as an important step forward. We stated then that we want to work directly with Congress to refine that proposal and to make sure that those dollars are provided in the most efficient and effective manner.

To that end, Senator, it is our belief that funding must be provided directly to the cities and counties as first responders, as you said in your opening statement, rather than flowing through the States as currently proposed by the administration. As we know, dialing 911 does not get you a State trooper.

Secondly, we must ensure that funding can be used to not only prepare for a possible attack, but also to help prevent future attacks. Our police departments must have access to funding, and officer deployments such as overtime should be specifically authorized.

For example, mayors call for and support the more detailed terrorist alert system unveiled by Governor Ridge, but these alerts will continue to require more officers on the streets; in essence, national security being provided by local law enforcement.

This is why the Conference of Mayors strongly supports legislation being sponsored by Senator Clinton and others to create a highly flexible homeland security block grant, the ongoing fight against crime, as you talked about, Senator. And let me address specifically the kinds of choices that face me. And you indicated in your chart that several areas have been cut, but let me add one more.

The public housing drug elimination program, administered by HUD, was eliminated last year. My city received $188,000 from our housing authority under this grant to operate three precinct stations located in our housing projects. All three now face elimination. This reduction, along with homeland security requirements, will make me choose between protecting my citizens against a terrorist who may attack my community and those terrorists or criminals who strike my city everyday.

The worst terrorist to most of us in America is the one who lives next door and who, through fear of daily crime, keeps you from living your life. Public safety is achieved by balancing of resources to needs, and every community is different. That is why, as we wage the new war against terrorism, we must not retreat from the ongoing fight against crime.

In the 1990s, mayors worked closely with our police chiefs and officers to increase public safety, with dramatic results, as indicated by your charts. As of last year, violent crime was estimated to be at a 20-year low nationwide. Mayors know that the major factors in this crime reduction were additional officers on the street, the deployment of new technology, and a new focus on community policing, all of which were greatly assisted by the COPS program and local law enforcement block grants.

Just last week, the Conference of Mayors sponsored an event in Baltimore which highlighted a 24-percent crime reduction in that city over the past 2 years. Baltimore Mayor O'Malley was emphatic: "This would not have been possible without the help of Federal resources." You will find similar stories in cities large and small all across this Nation.

But while there have been major reductions, crime is still a major issue in many cities and in many neighborhoods within those cities. In addition, we know that the key indicators, such as the economy and the return of more than 600,000 ex-convicts annually to our cities, have led experts to predict an upswing in crime rates.

Between 1993 and 2000, crime in North Little Rock, as the national average reflects, was down over 27 percent. But last year we received a 9-percent increase in our statistics—the largest single increase since I have been mayor of our community.

Many cities want to hire additional officers, move existing officers into the streets, and place new officers in schools. In addition, there is a major interest in new crime-fighting technologies. Let me add, for example, in Arkansas today our statewide newspaper announced, through Senator Hutchinson and Senator Lincoln, $645,043 in COPS grants to police departments in Arkadelphia, Arkansas; Prairie Grove, Arkansas; Stutgart, Arkansas; and the White County Sheriff's Office, to work with schools and community organizations against school-related crime. Senator Hutchinson, of Arkansas, is quoted as saying "Every child deserves the ability to learn absent the fear of violence."

Senator this is why I find it difficult, if not impossible, to understand that OMB is proposing to cut the COPS program by 80 percent and eliminate the block grant program by merging it into the State Byrne grant. This comes on top of a 25-percent reduction in the local block grant last year. We must ensure that cities have the resources needed to fight both the domestic war on terrorism and the continuing war against crime. We simply cannot rob Peter to pay Paul.

I want to thank the chairman for sponsoring bipartisan legislation, S. 924, to reauthorize the COPS program, and urge this subcommittee to help us ensure that both COPS and local law enforcement block grants are funded for this year.

Finally, I might add that we need a new communications system between Federal and local public safety officials, with a 24-hour threat assessment capability appropriate for sharing intelligence. Our discussions with the administration on this point have been constructive, but we want to ensure that any institutional barriers to greater intelligence-sharing by the Federal Government are addressed. As such, we urge passage of the Federal-Local Enforcement Sharing Partnership Act, S. 1615, which will allow the Federal Government to increase intelligence-sharing with local and State governments.

Senator, in conclusion, I would like to thank the subcommittee for this opportunity to testify. I look forward to continued discussions together as we work together to strengthen our mutual homeland defense.

Thank you very much.

[The prepared statement of Mayor Hays follows:]

TESTIMONY OF PATRICK HENRY HAYS, MAYOR OF NORTH LITTLE ROCK, AR, ON BEHALF OF THE UNITED STATES CONFERENCE OF MAYORS

Good afternoon. I am Patrick Hays, Mayor of North Little Rock, Arkansas. I have served as Mayor for over 13 years, starting in January of 1989. I am here today on behalf of The U.S. Conference of Mayors, for which I serve as a Trustee and member of the Executive Committee.

I want to thank Chairman Biden for calling today's hearing, as well as Senator Grassley and the entire Subcommittee.

Mayors have consistently attached a high priority to preparing our cities for the possibility of disasters—both natural and man made.

Now, in the wake of September 11 and the anthrax mailings, emergency management planning has been redoubled, and there have been significant new deployments of public safety resources.

The Conference of Mayors released a survey which found that from September 11, 2001 through the end of 2002, cities will spend an additional $2.6 billion on new homeland security priorities including equipment, overtime and training.

Mayors know the importance of public safety and are 100 percent committed to the homeland war against terrorism. But we must forge a new federal-local partnership to make sure that our domestic soldiers—police, fire, emergency workers and other city employees—have the resources needed for this new challenge.

This was the message mayors and police chiefs carried to Congress last week, and I want to thank Chairman Biden for participating in our discussions.

In October of 2001 the Conference of Mayors sponsored a Safety and Security Summit at which we developed a National Action Plan covering transportation security, emergency management, and law enforcement.

I ask that our plan be entered into the record, and would like to touch on several key points related to law enforcement.

SUPPORTING OUR FIRST RESPONDERS

First, at a January 24 White House meeting with 300 mayors President Bush announced his $3.5 billion first responders initiative, which we praised as an important step forward. As we stated then, we want to work directly with Congress to refine that proposal and make sure that those dollars are provided in the most efficient and effective manner.

To that end, it is our belief that funding must be provided directly to city and county first responders, rather than all flowing through the states as proposed by the Administration.

After all, a 9–1–1 call does not get a state trooper.

Second, we must ensure that the funding can be used to not only prepare for a possible attack, but to also help prevent future attacks. Our police departments must have access to the funding, and officer deployments such as overtime should be specifically authorized.

For example, mayors called for and support the more detailed terrorism alert system unveiled by Governor Ridge, but these alerts will continue to require more officers on the streets—in essence national security being provided by local law enforcement.

This is why the Conference of Mayors strongly supports legislation being sponsored by Senator Clinton and several other Senators to create a highly flexible Homeland Security Block Grant.

THE ONGOING FIGHT AGAINST CRIME

Let me address specifically the kind of local choices mayors face.

Last year the Public Housing Drug Elimination Program, run through HUD, was eliminated. My city received $188,000 from our housing authority under this grant to operate three precinct stations located in our housing projects. All three now face elimination.

This reduction, along with homeland security requirements, will make me choose between protecting my citizens against a terrorist who may attack my community, and those terrorists or criminals which strike my city every day.

The worst terrorist to most of America is the one who lives next door, and who through fear of daily crime keeps you from living your life.

Public safety is achieved by a balancing of resources to needs, and every community is different.

That is why as we wage the new war against terrorism, we must not retreat from the ongoing fight against crime.

In the 1990's, mayors worked closely with our policy chiefs and officers to increase public safety—with dramatic results. As of last year, violent crime was estimated to be at a 20-year low nationwide.

Mayors strongly believe that major factors in this crime reduction were additional officers on the streets, the deployment of new technology, and a new focus on community policing—all of which were greatly assisted by the COPS program and Local Law Enforcement Block Grant (LLEBG).

Just last week the Conference of Mayors sponsored an event in Baltimore which highlighted a 24 percent crime reduction in that city over the past two years. Baltimore Mayor O'Malley is emphatic that this would not have been possible without the help of these federal resources, and you would find similar stories in cities large and small across the Nation.

But while there have been major reductions, crime is still a major issue in many cities, and in many neighborhoods within cities.

In addition, we know that key indicators, such as the economy and return of more than 600,000 ex-convicts annually to our cities, have led some experts to predict an upswing in crime rates.

Many cities want to hire additional officers, move existing officers onto the streets, and place new officers in schools. In addition, there is a major interest in new crime fighting technologies.

That is why we find it counterintuitive that OMB is proposing to cut COPS by 80 percent and eliminate the block grant by merging it into the state Byrne Grant program. This comes on top of a 25 percent reduction in the local block grant last year.

We must ensure that cities have the resources needed to fight both the domestic war on terrorism and the continuing war against crime. We simply cannot "Rob Peter to Pay Paul."

I want to thank Chairman Biden for sponsoring bi-partisan legislation (S. 924) to reauthorize the COPS program, and urge this Subcommittee to help us ensure that both COPS and the Local Law Enforcement Block Grant are funded this year.

FEDERAL-LOCAL LAW ENFORCEMENT COOPERATION

Finally, we need a new communications system between federal and local public safety officials with a "24/7" threat assessment capability and appropriate sharing of intelligence.

Our discussions with the Administration on this have been constructive, but we want to ensure that any institutional barriers to greater intelligence sharing by the federal government are addressed.

That is why we urge passage of the "Federal-Local Information Sharing Partnership Act" (S. 1615) which would allow the federal government to increase intelligence sharing with local and state governments.

CONCLUSION

I want to thank the Subcommittee for this opportunity to testify, and I look forward to continued discussions as together we work to strengthen our Nation's homeland defense.

Chairman BIDEN. Thank you very much, Pat.

Mayor Hood, welcome.

STATEMENT OF HON. GLENDA E. HOOD, ORLANDO, FL, ON BEHALF OF THE NATIONAL LEAGUE OF CITIES

Mayor HOOD. Thank you, Mr. Chairman, and to you and members of the subcommittee I want to thank you for giving the National League of Cities an opportunity to testify today.

Mayor Hays and I work very closely on things between the U.S. Conference of Mayors and the League of Cities, so it is always good to share things with him. I think we are all aware that we are very pleased to have this opportunity because of the sharing of our position on homeland security and the imminent needs of our local law enforcement agencies.

The National League of Cities is the Nation's oldest national association that represents municipal interests in Washington. NLC's membership includes more than 18,000 cities, and it also has 135,000 mayors and local elected officials as its members.

At this time, I would ask that my written testimony be submitted for the record, with any additional letters and statements from my colleagues throughout the Nation who express strong bipartisan support for the Community-Oriented Policing Services program and the related programs that are extremely vital to our local public safety needs for crime prevention, for drug control, for technology deployment, for emergency communications, and new responsibilities for homeland security.

Chairman BIDEN. Without objection, it will be placed in the record.

Mayor HOOD. Thank you.

On behalf of NLC, I would like to express again my gratitude to you for introducing Senate bill 924. This reauthorization of the Community-Oriented Policing Services program is important to us, and to expand its purpose to include special assistance for small cities with populations of 50,000 or less and, of course, more funding for police officers hired through the universal hiring program, along with community-based prosecution programs and partnerships with schools and faith-based or religiously-affiliated organizations. Your longstanding leadership has certainly showed a commitment to ensuring that communities across the Nation are safe and secure, and I think that is everybody's goal.

The COPS program and other programs such as the local law enforcement block grant face significant changes in the administration's fiscal year 2003 budget proposal. Cities need vital funding for local public safety needs, and I can't underline and emphasize that enough. The National League of Cities believes it is imperative that Congress maintain level funding for these programs.

Since the COPS program was created in 1994, the Nation has experienced a 28-percent reduction in crime. Similarly, the local law enforcement block grant has helped fund numerous successful crime prevention programs that serve specific local needs for our

85-884 D-2

youth, for community organizations, for public safety technology, and for overtime pay for police officers in certain situations such as September 11.

The administration has proposed a first responder initiative that I know Mayor Hays spoke of, to fund needs for local and State emergency preparedness capacities and capabilities against terrorism, such as planning and equipment and training and exercises. This proposal should also address critical needs for crime prevention.

As NLC's current president Mayor Karen Anderson, of Minnetonka, Minnesota, whom you met with last week, Mr. Chairman, has stated, "There is more to homeland security than protecting against a terrorist attack. We need to work together to strengthen our homeland defenses and assess other long-term needs that will strengthen our communities."

Mayor Anderson goes on to say, "Let's make sure we don't rob Peter to pay Paul in fiscal year 2003 or beyond. Let's work together to find the right balance that takes into account the importance of investing in our cities and towns."

In this regard, the National League of Cities supports continued funding for community policing and the local law enforcement block grant. These programs should not be eliminated, especially when cities and towns of all sizes are facing severe budget constraints.

To the extent that the local law enforcement block grant and Byrne grant may be consolidated, it is critical that as many dollars as possible are sent to the local level, with as much flexibility as possible. These programs directly impact both local hometown security and national homeland security priorities. Again, I believe this is everyone's goal.

I don't have any props for you today, but I do have a lot of great examples, and I am going to start with my own city of Orlando. In Orlando, 103 police officers have been hired through the COPS program. The COPS technology program has funded 86 mobile data terminals and 13 specialized laptops to increase efficiency and to decrease response times in our community.

If overall COPS funding were reduced, I would be unable to put the officers on the streets as quickly as our growth needs demand that I do. I may even be put in the situation to reduce other fundamental public services to continue the community policing and crime prevention initiatives that have fostered that significant decrease in crime in my city. This is truly unacceptable, not only to my city but to all cities, especially when a majority of local and State budgets are in decline in many ways.

Let me give you another example in my own State of Florida, the city of Pembroke Pines. They have used the COPS funding for several initiatives to increase patrols around schools and businesses, to expand bicycle patrols to increase community contact with officers, to establish a community affairs unit, and to ensure more effective prosecution of cases through an enhanced records management system.

Mayor Alex Fekete stated that these initiatives would not have been possible without the financial impetus provided by the COPS grant awards. Any reduction, in Mayor's Fekete's mind, to the

COPS program in fiscal year 2003 could curtail further capabilities of his city to expand its community policing initiatives.

Another example is the city of Wichita, which has hired 125 police officers through the COPS program, and has experienced more than a 22-percent decline in crime since 1994. Former NLC president and mayor of Wichita, Bob Knight, stated that neighborhood associations and crime prevention partnerships have grown from only 8 to more than 80 since 1995.

"Community policing officers have played a significant role in bringing citizens together to identify safety and security issues," says Mayor Knight. He also says that the result has been the development of neighborhood associations that can form partnerships with businesses, with churches, with non-profit organizations, with governments, and with educational institutions to identify solutions for positive change.

His superintendent of public schools, Winston Brooks, noted that students and staff benefit daily from school resource officers who provide law-related educational programs, informal counseling sessions, mentoring and tutoring, and assistance with school safety and crisis response planning.

Another example is Mayor John DeStefano, whom you met with last week as well, from New Haven, Connecticut. He says he has experienced significant declines in all of the Part I crimes in his city since 1994. Homicides are down 42 percent, robberies have decreased by 33 percent, and motor vehicle thefts have declined by more than 59 percent. He noted that any loss of dollars for both technology and other competitive grants would negatively impact the city's police department, thereby preventing expanded partnerships with community groups and impeding the overall problem-solving capacity within his city.

"The proposed changes in the COPS would have a negative effect on our crime statistics," Police Chief Melvin Wearing, of New Haven, says. He says, "We have seen continued decreases since the program's inception, and we have been able to maintain those lower numbers as a result."

In the city of Hayward, California, they have implemented several crime prevention initiatives through the COPS program, including a successful community collaboration with neighborhood groups and other non-profit organizations. The Hayward Police Department also acquired 100 laptop computers, a new management information system, property and mapping modules, and network connection to State and Federal law enforcement networks through the technology component of the COPS program.

"If funding were reduced or eliminated, progress could be slowed significantly," according to council member Olden Henson. "Our ability to grow and adapt to the changing needs of our community would be negatively impacted without COPS-funded initiatives," he goes on to say.

The COPS program has also been vital in preventing the proliferation of gang activity and methamphetamine manufacturing and trafficking in the city of Watertown, South Dakota. Their mayor, Brenda Barger, says, "By hampering these two ills in the community, we have managed to prevent the collateral effects, such as robbery, assault, and other crimes." "Since we have hired the additional officers," she says, "we have enhanced crime prevention efforts by adding bike patrols, crime-free multi-housing initiatives, a school resource officer, a very effective accident reduction program, and recruitment of community-oriented officers through COPS training for supervisors."

"On a day-to-day basis," Mayor Barger says, "officers have more time to interact and assimilate with the community they serve. I feel that our policing style has contributed greatly to the quality of life in our community. The result of elimination would be rather obvious, and it would be obvious very quickly. Programs would have to be cut. Crime would again begin to increase. Quality of life in the community would decline."

Well, Mr. Chairman, I think these are just a few examples that represent the thousands of successful crime prevention initiatives that have been funded by the COPS program. Our country, especially now, needs community policing. It is something that we all believe in and it is something that we have all depended upon.

The best way to ensure domestic safety is through continued community partnerships, through problem-solving and enhanced communication that COPS indeed has facilitated since 1994. Full funding for COPS and other public safety programs must continue to be a cornerstone in effective law enforcement over the next several years as we face those many domestic challenges that lie ahead.

I greatly appreciate your leadership on this issue, and on behalf of NLC thank you. We certainly look forward to working with you and the House and Senate Appropriations Committees as the fiscal year 2003 budget process moves forward to ensure full funding for local public safety programs.

Thank you.

Chairman BIDEN. Mayor, thank you very much. I am going to come back to questions, but out of curiosity, has Orlando's population shrunk since you have been mayor?

Mayor HOOD. No.

Chairman BIDEN. Has it grown?

Mayor HOOD. Yes.

Chairman BIDEN. Most cities, particularly larger cities, but all cities, end up being the repository for an increasingly large number of dependent people; that is, people with lower incomes, people dependent on various programs to make their minimum subsistence. Have you had any change in the make-up of your city that way, or is it the same? Have those living at the poverty level or below the poverty level increased or decreased? Do you know, off the top of your head?

Mayor HOOD. Slight fluctuations, but nothing major.

Chairman BIDEN. Yes.

Mayor HOOD. Of course, in our situation we have over 40 million visitors a year. So that is kind of a phenomenon that we have that many other cities don't have.

Chairman BIDEN. Which was the third thing I was going to ask you. Nonetheless, your crime rate went down?

Mayor HOOD. Yes.

Chairman BIDEN. Astounding.

[The prepared statement of Mayor Hood follows:]

STATEMENT OF THE HONORABLE GLENDA E. HOOD, MAYOR OF ORLANDO, FL, ON BEHALF OF THE NATIONAL LEAGUE OF CITIES

Chairman Biden and Members of the Subcommittee, the National League of Cities (NLC) is pleased to have this opportunity to share its position on homeland security and the imminent needs of our local law enforcement agencies. I am Glenda Hood, Mayor of Orlando, Florida, and Past President of the National League of Cities.

The National League of Cities is the nation's oldest national association representing municipal interests in Washington. NLC's membership includes more than 18,000 cities and towns across the country, with over 135,000 mayors and local elected officials.

At this time, I ask that my written testimony be submitted for the record with additional letters and statements from my colleagues throughout the nation who express strong bipartisan support for the Community Oriented Policing Services (COPS) program and related programs that are extremely vital to local public safety needs for crime prevention, drug control, technology deployment, emergency communications, and new responsibilities for homeland security.

On behalf of NLC, I would like to express my gratitude to you, Mr. Chairman, for introducing S. 924, the PROTECTION ACT (Providing Reliable Officers, Technology, Education, Community Prosecutors, and Training In Our Neighborhoods Act) to reauthorize the Community Oriented Policing Services Program and expand its purpose to include special assistance for small cities with populations of 50,000 or less; more funding for retention of police officers hired through the Universal Hiring Program; community-based prosecution programs; and partnerships with schools and religiously-affiliated organizations. Your long-standing leadership on this issue clearly shows your commitment to ensuring that communities across the nation are safe and secure.

As you know, the COPS program, and other programs such as the Local Law Enforcement Block Grant, face significant changes in the Administration's fiscal year 2003 budget proposal. Cities need vital funding for local public safety needs. The National League of Cities believes it is imperative that Congress maintain level funding for these programs.

Since the COPS program was created in 1994, the nation has experienced a 28 percent reduction in crime. Similarly, the Local Law Enforcement Block grant has helped fund numerous successful crime prevention programs that serve specific local needs for youth, community organizations, public safety technology and overtime pay for police officers in certain situations such as September 11.

The Administration has proposed a First Responder Initiative to fund needs for local and state emergency preparedness capabilities against terrorism—such as planning, equipment, training and exercises. This proposal should also address critical needs for crime prevention.

As NLC's current President, Mayor Karen Anderson of Minnetonka, Minnesota, has stated, "There's more to homeland security than protecting against a terrorist attack. We need to work together to strengthen our homeland defenses and assess other long-term needs that will strengthen our communities. Let's make sure we don't rob Peter to pay Paul in FY 2003 or beyond. Let's work together to find the right balance that takes into account the importance of investing in our cities and towns."

In this regard, NLC supports continued funding for community policing and the Local Law Enforcement Block Grant. These programs should not be eliminated, especially when cities and towns of all sizes are facing severe budget constraints because of the recession and unforeseen consequences of the September 11 terrorist attacks. To the extent the Local Law Enforcement Block Grant and Byrne Grant are consolidated, it is critical that as many dollars as possible are sent to the local levels with as much flexibility as possible. These programs directly impact both local hometown security and national homeland security priorities.

For example, the proposed changes in the COPS program would eliminate funding for hiring and retention of police officers, school resource officers, and targeted crime prevention grant programs for small communities.

In my City of Orlando, 103 police officers have been hired through the COPS program. The COPS technology program, Making Officer Redeployment Effective, has funded 86 mobile data terminals and 13 specialized laptops to increase efficiency and decrease response times. If overall COPS funding were reduced, I would be unable to put officers on the streets as quickly as our growth needs demand; and I may be put in the position to reduce other fundamental public services to continue the community policing and crime prevention initiatives that have fostered a significant decrease in crime. This is unacceptable to our cities, especially when a majority of local and state budgets are in a serious decline.

The City of Pembroke Pines, Florida, has used COPS funding for several initiatives to increase patrols around schools and businesses; expand bicycle patrols to increase community contact with officers; establish a Community Affairs Unit; and ensure more effective prosecution of cases through an enhanced records management system. Mayor Alex Fekete stated that these initiatives would not have been possible without the financial impetus provided by the COPS grant awards. Any reduction of the COPS Program in FY 2003 could curtail any further capabilities of the City to expand its community policing initiatives.

The City of Wichita has hired 125 police officers through the COPS program, and has experienced more than a 22 percent decline in crime since 1994. Former NLC President and Mayor of Wichita, Bob Knight, stated that neighborhood associations and crime prevention partnerships have grown from only eight to more than eighty since 1995. "Community policing officers have played a significant role in brining citizens together to identify safety and security issues. The result has been the development of neighborhood associations that can form partnerships with businesses, churches, non-profit agencies, government, and educational institutions to identify solutions for positive change."

Winston Brooks, Superintendent of Wichita Public Schools, noted that students and staff benefit daily from school resource officers who provide law related educational programs, informal counseling, mentoring, tutoring, and assistance with school safety and crisis response planning.

The City of New Haven, Connecticut, has experienced significant declines in all Part I crimes since 1994. For example, homicides are down by 42 percent; robberies have decreased by 33 percent; and motor vehicle thefts have declined by more than 59 percent. NLC First Vice President and Mayor John DeStefano noted that the loss of dollars for both technology and other competitive grants would negatively impact the City's police department, preventing expanded partnerships with community groups and impeding the overall problem-solving capacity. The proposed changes in the COPS program would have a "negative effect on our crime statistics," Police Chief Melvin Wearing stated. "We have seen continued decreases since the program's inception, and we have been able to maintain the lower numbers."

The City of Hayward, California, has implemented several crime prevention initiatives through the COPS program including a successful Community Collaborative with neighborhood groups and other non-profit organizations. The Hayward Police Department also acquired 100 laptop computers, a new management information system, property and mapping modules, and a network connection to state and federal law enforcement networks through the technology components of the COPS program. "If funding were reduced or eliminated, progress could be slowed significantly, according to Councilmember Olden Henson. "Our ability to grow and adapt to the changing needs of our community would be negatively impacted without COPS-funded initiatives."

The COPS program has been vital in preventing the proliferation of gang activity, and methamphetamines manufacturing and trafficking in the City of Watertown, South Dakota. "By hampering these two ills in our community, we have managed to prevent the collateral effects such as robbery, assault, and other crimes," said Mayor Brenda Barger. "Since we have hired the additional officers, we have enhanced crime prevention efforts by adding bike patrols, crime free multi-housing initiatives, a school resource officer, a very effective accident reduction program, and recruitment of community oriented officers through COPS training for supervisors.

"On a day-to-day basis, the officers have more time to interact and assimilate with the community they serve," Mayor Barger continued. "I feel that our policing style has contributed greatly to the quality of life in our community. The result of elimination would be obvious rather quickly. Programs would have to be cut. Crime would again begin to increase. Quality of life in the community would decline."

Mr. Chairman, these examples represent the thousands of successful crime prevention initiatives funded by the COPS program. The country—especially now—needs community policing. The best way to ensure domestic safety is through the continued community partnerships, problem solving, and enhanced communication that COPS has facilitated since 1994. Full funding for COPS and other public safety programs must continue to be a cornerstone in effective law enforcement over the next several years as we face the domestic challengers ahead.

Mr. Chairman and Members of the Subcommittee, I greatly appreciate your leadership on this issue, and look forward to working with you and the House and Senate Appropriations Committees as the fiscal year 2003 budget process moves forward to ensure full funding for local public safety programs. I would be happy to answer any questions that the Subcommittee may have at the appropriate time.

Thank you.

Chairman BIDEN. Chief Szczerba, welcome. The floor is yours.

STATEMENT OF MICHAEL J. SZCZERBA, CHIEF OF POLICE, WILMINGTON POLICE DEPARTMENT, WILMINGTON, DE

Chief SZCZERBA. Good afternoon, Senator. I was a little uneasy speaking here today, after you lined me up with mayors, I don't know what Mayor Baker is going to think when I get back home.

Chairman BIDEN. You will be fine.

Chief SZCZERBA. I would like to thank you for inviting me here to speak today on this very important issue.

For the record, my name is Chief Michael Szczerba. I am the chief in the city of Wilmington, Delaware. I haven't brought any props either today, but I did bring along with me my deputy chief, Inspector James Wright.

Chairman BIDEN. Inspector, welcome.

Chief SZCZERBA. Like the sheriff, he is also a lieutenant colonel in our Delaware National Guard. Hopefully, this time next year I will address him as "colonel."

The Wilmington Department of Police has an authorized strength of 289 officers. We are tasked with the job of policing a city of about 14 square miles. We have a residential population of 75,000 people, and that number probably doubles during our business hours.

In 1996, the city of Wilmington experienced once of its worst economic downturns in recent history. This crisis affected every aspect of the city's budget, including that of the police department. Through retirement incentives and attrition, the Department of Police in Wilmington reached an all-time low in staffing, with the numbers plummeting to 221 officers. And I would emphasize that was 221 officers on paper.

Along with this decrease in manpower, the city experienced one of the most catastrophic increases in gun violence to date. In 1996, we saw a record number of 108 shootings and 21 homicides in a city that prior to that never saw more than 40 shootings or 12 homicides annually. Our city was under siege, and staffing was so low that neighboring police agencies offered their personnel and resources to help the city combat this growing epidemic.

Through the Biden crime law—and that is how we know it in Delaware still—the Department of Police was able to hire 28 officers through the use of Federal funds. These Federal funds replaced resources that our city just did not have. The assistance from the Biden crime law, as we call it in Delaware, did not end there. On October 3, you and then-Mayor James Sills, and Police Chief Michael Boykin announced a comprehensive crime-fighting plan, dubbed Operation Quiet Storm, which was based on strategies employed in other large cities nationally that had reduced crime rates significantly.

Operation Quiet Storm was designed to storm five identified crime hot spots with local law enforcement resources working in concert with Federal law enforcement agencies to attack the problems of gangs, guns, and drugs. With numbers back to its authorized strength, the Wilmington Department of Police acted as the lead agency in this effort, resulting in cutting the amount of shootings in half and decreasing homicides by 40 percent.

This is just one example of the impact that the crime law has had on local law enforcement agencies. Speaking specifically for the city of Wilmington, the funds procured through the local law enforcement block grant provided by the crime law has allowed the Wilmington Department of Police to increase its services to the city of Wilmington by increasing current programs and reinstituting programs that had been cut due to budget constraints.

For example, as a result, we were able to expand our K–9 unit from 6 to 10 officers. Our crime prevention unit, which instills community-oriented policing, suffered from budget cuts, yet remains a constant request from our residents and our business folks. That was re-funded and is now providing an invaluable service to help people take proactive steps to protect themselves.

We have increased our computer systems and our forensic technology, including the purchasing of an IBIS system, or Ceasefire. Wilmington is only one of about 20 sites in 12 States throughout the country to have this sophisticated, computerized, digitized weapon and bullet identification system. The system is designed to cease the escalating and alarming number of gun-related crimes and homicides in Wilmington and other cities throughout the country, and it has had a positive impact on our investigative techniques.

One of the best aspects of the local law enforcement block grant is allowing the Department of Police to institute anti-drug patrols in areas that have been torn apart by the scourge of drugs.

As the climate in this country has changed, attention must be placed on homeland security. However, homeland security has a two-pronged definition, the first being the most obvious, and that is taking measures to ensure that the tragedies that affected this country never occur again.

The second is providing the security of those who live day to day in our cities and communities. The onus of that security falls on us in local law enforcement. The Biden crime law has made it possible for us to allow the quality of life in all of our cities and communities to increase, as the national crime trends have decreased.

In these hard times where some communities like the city of Wilmington are reaching economic hardships, homeland security comes in the form of our front-line officers, who rely in part on the resources provided by the COPS office. I fear that if these resources are restricted, history will repeat itself. I fear that police manpower will decrease, allowing gun violence to increase and terrorists that take the form of drug dealers will flourish.

If this occurs, the quality of life in our communities, the real infrastructure of this country, will decrease greatly, undoing all the good that this crime law has done, as well as the hard work of all police officers in this country.

I have provided a copy of what I have spoken on today for the record. It is also provided on disk, and I will be happy to answer any questions.

[The prepared statement of Chief Szczerba follows:]

Good afternoon Senators and Chairman Biden. I would like to thank you, Chairman Biden, for inviting me here to speak today on this very important issue. My name is Chief Michael J. Szczerba, Chief of the Wilmington Department of Police in the State of Delaware. Accompanying me is my Deputy Chief, Inspector James Wright. The Department of Police has an authorized strength of 289 sworn Officers, tasked with policing a city of 14 square miles, and a residential population of 75,000 people, with that number doubling during business hours. In 1996, the City of Wilmington experienced one of its worst economic downturn in recent times. The crisis affected every aspect of the City's budget, including that of the Police Department. Through retirement incentives and attrition, the Department of Police reached an all time low of staffing, with numbers plummeting to 221 sworn Officers. Along with this decrease in manpower, the City experienced the most catastrophic increase in gun violence to date. 1996 saw a record number 108 shootings and 21 homicides in a city that prior to that year never saw more than 40 shootings and 12 homicides annually. Our city was under siege, and staffing was so low that neighboring Police Agencies offered their personnel and resources to help Wilmington combat this growing epidemic.

Through the Biden Crime Law, the Department of Police was able to hire 28 Officers through the use of federal funds. These federal funds replaced resources that our city just did not have. But assistance from the Biden Crime Law, as we affectionately call it in Delaware, did not end there. On October 3, 1997, Senator Biden, then Wilmington Mayor James H. Sills, Jr., and then Police Chief Michael Boykin announced a comprehensive crime-fighting plan, dubbed "Operation Quiet Storm," which was based on strategies employed in other large cities nationally that had reduced crime rates significantly. "Operation Quiet Storm" was designed to storm five identified crime hot spots with local law enforcement resources working in concert with federal law enforcement agencies to attack the problems of gangs, guns and drugs. With numbers now back to its authorized strength, the Wilmington Department of Police acted as the lead agency in this joint effort, resulting in cutting the amount of shootings in half, and decreasing homicides by 40 percent.

This is just one but important example of the impact that the Biden Crime Law has had on local law enforcement agencies. Speaking specifically for the City of Wilmington, the funds procured through the Local Law Enforcement Block Grant provided by the Biden Crime Law has allowed the Wilmington Department of Police to increase its services to the citizens of the City of Wilmington by increasing current programs and reinstituting programs that had been cut due to budget restraints. As a result, we were able to expand our K–9 Unit from 6 Officers to 10 Officers. Our Crime Prevention Unit, which instills Community Oriented Policing, suffered from budget cuts yet remained a constant request of residents, was refunded and is now providing an invaluable service to help people take proactive steps to protect themselves. We have increased our computer systems and our forensic technology, including the purchasing of the IBIS system, or "Ceasefire". Wilmington is one of only about 20 sites in 12 states throughout the country to have this sophisticated, computerized, digitized weapon and bullet identification system. This system is designed to cease the escalating and alarming number of gun-related crimes and homicides in Wilmington and other cities throughout this country, and it has had a positive impact on investigative techniques. One of the best aspects of the Local Law Enforcement Block Grant is it allowing the Department of Police to institute Anti-Drug Patrols in areas that had been torn apart by the scourge of drugs.

As the climate in this country has changed, attention must be placed on Homeland Security. However, Homeland Security has a two-pronged definition. The first being the most obvious . . . taking measures to ensure that the tragedies that affected this country never occur again. The second is providing the security of those who live day to day in our cities and communities. The onus of that security falls on those of us in local law enforcement. The Biden Crime Law has made it possible for us to allow the quality of life in all of our cities and communities to increase as national crime trends have decreased. In these hard times where some communities, like the City of Wilmington, are reaching economic hardships, that Homeland Security which comes in the form of our frontline Police Officers, relies in part, on the resources provided by the Cops Office. I fear that if these resources are restricted, history will repeat itself. I fear that Police manpower will decrease, allowing gun violence to increase and the terrorists that take the form of drug dealers will flourish. If this occurs, the quality of life of our communities, the real infrastructure of this country, will decrease exponentially, undoing all the good that the Biden Crime Law has done as well the hard work of the Police Officers in this country.

Chairman BIDEN. Thank you very much, Chief. I appreciate your testimony.

Mr. Johnson.

STATEMENT OF WILLIAM J. JOHNSON, EXECUTIVE DIRECTOR, NATIONAL ASSOCIATION OF POLICE ORGANIZATIONS, WASHINGTON, DC

Mr. JOHNSON. Thank you, Mr. Chairman. I appreciate the opportunity to speak before your subcommittee today. I have also provided copies of my written testimony and would respectfully ask at the outset that it be included.

Chairman BIDEN. It will be placed in the record in full.

Mr. JOHNSON. Thank you, sir.

Mr. Chairman, and to your committee, on behalf of the 220,000 rank-and-file police officers from all across the United States, I would like to thank you for this opportunity to testify today on our Nation's homeland defense and the needs of local law enforcement.

The National Association of Police Organizations, or NAPO, is surprised and is frankly truly concerned about the administration's proposed fiscal year 2003 budget and its intended future, or lack thereof, for the Community-Oriented Policing Services, or COPS, program presented administered by the United States Department of Justice.

Today, I would like to discuss three paramount concerns that NAPO has regarding the administration's proposed budget and its effects. These are: the future of the COPS program, the grant funds overseen presently by the Office of Justice Assistance, and the status of State and local law enforcement in the war on terrorism in light of the administration's proposed movement of supervision of Federal assistance from the Department of Justice to the Federal Emergency Management Agency.

Created by the 1994 crime bill, as you well know, the COPS Office has funded the hiring of over 110,000 police officers in more than 11,000 communities across the United States. In addition, it has contributed countless resources, including enhanced crime-fighting technology and the development of innovative partnerships with communities, to fight crime.

Both the public and Congress recognized the benefits of putting more cops on the streets. These benefits have been further demonstrated more recently in the 2001 study at the University of Nebraska authored by Dr. Jihong Zhao which correlated the steady decline of violent crime throughout the United States over the last few years with the success of the COPS program. In fact, the charts that your staff has provided today demonstrate the same thing. This study was presented to the Subcommittee on Crime at a hearing held on December 5, 2001.

Despite the tremendous impact this program has had throughout the country, the administration's proposed fiscal year 2003 would effectively gut the COPS program and end the instrumental practice of adding new officers to the street. As you have pointed out, Mr. Chairman, it is very similar to cutting the grass one time and then sitting back and saying, well, I don't need the lawnmower anymore, except in this case what the administration, with all due respect, is doing is not putting it in the garage. They are throwing away the lawnmower and giving the money for a new one to the neighbor who has never seen one or knows what it is used for.

NAPO represents the police forces of some of our Nation's largest cities. Therefore, we researched in preparation for today's hearing what effect the termination of the COPS program would have on the needs of some of these local law enforcement agencies.

Since 1994, the city of Los Angeles has been awarded funding for the new hiring or redeployment of more than 3,700 officers, put on its streets.

Chairman BIDEN. An additional 3,700.

Mr. JOHNSON. Yes, sir, yes, above and beyond what they had, more than 3,700. In funding, this has been just over $298 million allocated to meet the requested technology and hiring needs of Los Angeles' local law enforcement.

Over the same period, Miami-Dade County has benefitted from the addition of more than 1,100 new or redirected officers and the allocation of over $84 million for hiring and technological needs.

The city of Chicago has gained more than 1,500 new officers and over $104 million, and the city of New York has benefitted from the addition of more than 7,300 new officers on the streets and over $529 million in needed improvements funding. These cities have also all seen a directly correlated and substantial reduction in crime since the mid-1990s.

I would just point out that in New York City, that figure of more than 7,300 is about 18 percent of their force. They have got about 39,000 sworn officers. About 18 percent of those are COPS officers, thanks to the bill that you authored.

As you also have pointed out today, in a time when our country is necessarily focused on homeland defense, we believe the COPS program just be an intrinsic part of any defense plan because it has a proven effect on crime reduction. This is why COPS is of such importance now. It will help protect our communities by increasing, and more often maintaining, the needed police presence on our streets, while public safety services are stretched and redefined to confront the ever-changing threat of terrorism.

Our national president, Tom Scotto, who is a New York City detective whom you know and many members of the committee know, was telling me just this morning that it has not just been since September 11, but since then it has been unrelenting and continuous drain upon every aspect of law enforcement in that city.

Immediately, in the aftermath of the morning of September 11 and through to today, all the other sites, such as the Statue of Liberty, the UN Building, the Brooklyn Bridge, the various tunnels, the power plants, the water plants, are now designated sites that law enforcement has to cover in a way that they didn't have to before. The fact that manpower must be diverted to these new sites takes other cops off the street from their regular duties.

A second concern NAPO has regarding the administration's proposed fiscal year 2003 budget is the changes called for in the block grant and Byrne State and local law enforcement assistance grants, which are presently run by the Department of Justice's Office of Justice Assistance. These two grant programs have had a positive effect in strengthening law enforcement's ability to reduce crime and fund programs that make a difference in the community.

The administration has proposed consolidating these two grant programs along with other smaller programs into a new justice assistance grant program. While the block grants and Byrne received a combined funding of over $1 billion in fiscal year 2001, the new condensed grant program would be funded at a much smaller dollar level, while being asked at the same time to cover more outlets. The outcome will be less available funds to assist local law enforcement at a time when public safety budgets are being overrun by new national security concerns.

A third major concern that NAPO has over the administration's proposed budget is the movement of monies and supervision from the Department of Justice's Office of Justice Programs to the Federal Emergency Management Agency. Please do not understand this as an overly negative criticism of FEMA. FEMA can provide a valuable service to communities beaten down by disaster and can assist in their quick rehabilitation.

But NAPO's concern consists in the fact that in this new war on terrorism, the administration wishes to move police interests from a body that has fostered 30 years of working relations with local police to a body that has never dealt with the needs of police before. As President Lincoln said, during wartime you don't change your horse midstream. It would be foolish to invite an internecine bureaucratic power struggle in the midst of an ongoing shooting war.

While the needs of police officers as first responders are similar in some ways to fire and emergency services, they are vastly different in other ways. An agency like the Department of Justice, with 30 years of hard-won experience on what police need and how best to allocate it to them, should not be displaced by an agency with whom law enforcement has no such prior experience. We would be very disappointed if law enforcement lost such a great tool in its fight against crime.

Our concerns are three-fold, then, when we look at the administration's proposed budget: the future of the COPS program, the future of the grant funding, and the need to keep the Department of Justice as the agency of record for the needs of law enforcement.

Our country has entered a time of challenge, but it is not a time of insurmountable crisis. Now is when the tools that have proven to be so effective have to be brought out, and even enhanced, so that the job we face as a Nation can be done, and done right the first time.

Thank you, Mr. Chairman.

[The prepared statement of Mr. Johnson follows:]

TESTIMONY BY WILLIAM J. JOHNSON, EXECUTIVE DIRECTOR OF THE NATIONAL ASSOCIATION OF POLICE ORGANIZATIONS

Mr. Chairman, Senator Grassley, members of the Senate Subcommittee, My name is William J. Johnson and I am the Executive Director of the National Association of Police Organizations. NAPO is a coalition of police unions and associations from across the United States that serves here in Washington, DC to advance the interests of America's law enforcement through legislative and legal advocacy.

On behalf of 220,000 rank-and-file police officers from across the United States, I would like to thank you for this opportunity to testify today on our Nation's homeland defense and the needs of law enforcement. NAPO is surprised and truly concerned about the Administration's proposed 2003 fiscal budget and its intended future for the Community Oriented Policing Service program (COPS), administered by the Department of Justice.

Today, I will discuss three paramount concerns NAPO has on the Administration's proposed budget. These are the future of the COPS program. The beneficial grant funds overseen by the Office of Justice Assistance and the status of state and local law enforcement in the war on terrorism in light of the Administration's proposed movement of supervision from the Department of Justice to the Federal Emergency Management Agency.

Created by the 1994 Crime bill, the COPS Office has funded the hiring of over 110,000 police officers in 11,300 communities. In addition, it has contributed countless resources, including enhanced crime-fighting technology and the development of innovative partnerships with communities to fight crime.

Both the public and Congress recognize the benefits of putting more cops on the street. As it has been often and rightly said, once you've finished cutting the grass, you don't throw away the lawn mower.

These benefits have been further demonstrated in the 2001 study by the University of Nebraska, authored by Dr. Jihong Zhao, which correlated the steady decline of violent crime over the last few years with the success of this program. This study was presented to the Senate Subcommittee on Crime hearing held on December 5, 2001.

Despite the tremendous impact this program has had throughout the country the Administration's proposed FY 2003 budget would effectively gut the COPS program and end the instrumental practice of adding new officers to the streets.

As NAPO represents the police forces of some of our nation's largest cities, we researched what effect the termination of the COPS program would have on the needs of some of NAPO's local law enforcement agencies.

Per current information from the COPS office, since 1944 the City of Los Angeles has been awarded funding for the new hiring or redeployment of 3,731 officers to protect its streets. In funding, this has been just over 298 million dollars allocated to meet the requested technology and hiring needs of Los Angeles local law enforcement. Over the same period, the City of Miami has benefited from the addition of 1,184 new or redirected officers and the allocation of over 84 million dollars for hiring and technological needs. The City of Chicago has gained 1,593 Officers and over 104 million dollars and the City of New York has benefited from the addition of 7,356 officers to the street and over 529 million dollars in needed improvements funding. These cities have also seen a directly related and substantial reduction in crime since the mid 1990's

These figures represent what has already been allocated and we can only hope that these fundings are protected from proposed changes. More importantly these figures demonstrate that the future needs for these cities will no longer be addressed if the COPS program is dissolved.

In a time when our country is necessarily focused on homeland defense, we believe the COPS program must be an intrinsic part of any defense plan because it has a proven effect on crime reduction. This is why COPS is of such importance now. It will help protect our communities by increasing, and more often maintaining, the needed police presence on our streets while public safety services are stretched and re-defined to confront the ever changing threat of terrorism.

A second concern NAPO has over the Administrations proposed FY 2003 budget are the changes called for to the Local Law Enforcement Block Grant Program and the Byrne State and Local Law Enforcement Assistance Grants, which are run by the Department of Justice's Office of Justice Assistance. These two block grants have had a historically positive effect in strengthening law enforcement's ability to reduce crime and fund programs that make a difference in the community.

The Local Law Enforcement Block Grant Program has supported police by facilitating the hiring and training of new officers, paying overtime and procuring needed equipment and technology. LLEBG Funds also go to enhancing school safety, supporting drug courts, securing violent crime convictions, enhancing community policing and defraying the costs of officer insurances.

LLEBG funding commenced in 1996 and awarded over 450 million dollars in FY2001. Since its inception the grant has provided two and one half billion dollars in needed support to local law enforcement, money we could not have done without.

Much like the LLEGB, the Byrne Grant has awarded monies to assist educational and training programs for criminal justice personnel and has provided for technical assistance to state and local law enforcement. The Byrne Grant awarded over 524 million dollars in FY2001 and has provided over five and one half billion dollars since 1990.

The Administration has proposed consolidating these two grant programs, along with other smaller programs, into a new Justice Assistance Grant Program. While LLEGB and Byrne received a combined funding of over one billion dollars in FY 2001, this new condensed grant program would be funded at a smaller 800 million dollar level while being asked to cover more outlets. The outcome will be less available funds to assist law enforcement in a time when public safety budgets are being overrun by new national security concerns.

A third concern NAPO's has over the Administrations proposed FY 2003 budget is the movement of monies and supervision from the Department of Justice and Office of Justice Programs to the Federal Emergency Management Agency. Please do not misunderstand this as an overly negative criticism. FEMA can provide a valuable service to communities beaten down by disaster and can assist in their quick rehabilitation.

NAPO's concern consists in the fact that in this new war on terrorism, the Administration wishes to move police interests from a body that has fostered 30 years of working relations to a body that has never dealt with the needs of police before. As President Lincoln said, during wartime you don't change your horse in mid stream. Further, we would say, you don't cut the grass once and then give away your lawn mower to a neighbor who doesn't know what it's for or how to use it.

While the needs of police officers as first responders are similar in some ways to fire and Emergency Service, they are vastly different in other ways. An agency who has developed 30 years of knowledge on what police need and how best to allocate it to them should not be sidelined by an agency with whom law enforcement has had no prior experience. We would be very disappointed if law enforcement lost such a great tool in its fight against crime.

Senators, our concerns are three fold when we look at the Administration's proposed budget: The future of the COPS program; the future of beneficial grant funding; and the need to keep the Department of Justice as the agency of record for the needs of law enforcement. Our country has entered a time of challenge but it is not a time of insurmountable crises. Now is when the tools that have proven to be effective have to be brought out and even enhanced so the job can be done and done right the first time. I want to thank Chairman Biden and the Subcommittee members for this opportunity to voice the concerns of America's police and I respectfully request that my remarks be included in the record.

Chairman BIDEN. Thank you very much, Bill.

Sheriff.

STATEMENT OF TOMMY FERRELL, FIRST VICE PRESIDENT, NATIONAL SHERIFFS' ASSOCIATION, NATCHEZ, MS

Sheriff FERRELL. Thank you, Mr. Chairman. I, too, appreciate the opportunity and thank you for the invitation today.

I am Sheriff Tommy Ferrell, from Adams County, Mississippi, and I appear before you as the first vice president of the National Sheriffs' Association.

Chairman BIDEN. Sheriff, out of curiosity—I know your State—where is your county in the State, north, south?

Sheriff FERRELL. Down in the extreme southwest, right on the Mississippi-Louisiana border.

Chairman BIDEN. Thank you.

Sheriff FERRELL. And I invite you to visit.

Chairman BIDEN. Well, my daughter is down in New Orleans, just across the river there. I may need your help. We may have to invade New Orleans before it is over.

Sheriff FERRELL. I think we can take care of that, Senator.

Chairman BIDEN. She is at Tulane University.

Sheriff FERRELL. Good luck, sir. [Laughter.]

Chairman BIDEN. Believe me, I understand. She is a junior. Thank God, she is doing well, but I don't think she is going to come home. Maybe she won't come home. She is going to be bringing home somebody who talks like you and I am going to have to learn to speak southern all over again. Jim Eastland taught me and I am trying to learn again.

Sheriff FERRELL. Please don't take offense, sir, but if she finishes in New Orleans, she won't talk like she is from Delaware.

Chairman BIDEN. That is exactly right. [Laughter.]

Sheriff FERRELL. We are glad to have her in our area.

Chairman BIDEN. So am I. I am glad to have her there.

Sheriff FERRELL. I am here representing the sheriffs of the United States. I am the first vice president, and I will be sworn as president of the National Sheriffs' Association in June.

The National Sheriffs' Association is surprised and deeply concerned about the proposal by OMB to eliminate the Office of Domestic Preparedness, ODP, at the U.S. Justice Department, and to shift these responsibilities to the Federal Emergency Management Agency, FEMA.

This is a time when the American people need continuity and coordination, not the disruption of unnecessary reorganization. For this reason, I appear before you today to add the voice of the Nation's sheriffs to other law enforcement organizations that likewise oppose this OMB proposal. While we appreciate the efforts of OMB to consolidate functions and enhance efficiency, this proposal would unintentionally undermine the efforts of American law enforcement.

I will submit for the record a formal resolution adopted by the National Sheriffs Association earlier this month in which we set forth the reasons for our opposition to the proposed reorganization.

Let me explain the reasons for our opposition to the OMB proposal.

Experience with counter-terrorism: Sheriffs have worked with the Department of Justice on funding for anti-crime efforts since the Safe Streets Crime Act of 1968. Over these 34 years, the Department of Justice has established expertise that cannot be replicated by an agency that is new to law enforcement. Nothing more needs to be said other than it is apparent that there is no substitute for these 34 years of relationships and experience.

Contradiction of the PATRIOT Act: The sheriffs of our Nation applaud your courage and leadership in passing the PATRIOT, but we are confused by the OMB proposal, since it seems to repeal sections of the PATRIOT Act even before some of those provisions have been implemented.

For example, the OMB proposal seems to rewrite sections 1005 and 1014, which direct the Attorney General, not FEMA, to make grants to sheriffs for first responders, terrorism prevention, and anti-terrorism training. Law enforcement responds to a deadly threat, not FEMA. Look at the record of terrorist attacks around the globe. Terrorists attack with automatic weapons, bombs, and often take hostages. Side by side with Federal law enforcement, we will face the terrorists most probably with deadly weapons.

We will never ask nor can we expect our fire, EMS, or health personnel to face gunfire, explosives, or other deadly assaults. This is the job sheriffs and police, and it is ours alone. Once the threat has been addressed and public safety has been restored, only then is it possible to turn over the same to the FEMA agency. To do anything else would be contrary to a sheriff's oath of office and contrary to the laws of the States. To subordinate our crisis response to FEMA would compromise the statutory obligation of law enforcement officials to protect their communities.

Mr. Chairman, the House Subcommittee on Crime said it best in recognizing that this is the reality of both policy and practice across the Nation. They said, "The committee is concerned that FEMA is not the appropriate agency for these responsibilities. A terrorist attack is a criminal event, not a natural disaster."

The FEMA role is limited to consequences management. The prevention, detention, and apprehension of terrorists are law enforcement functions, and it is not appropriate for training and coordination to be assigned to the FEMA regime, where there are no such responsibilities. If there were to be another terrorist attack, responding to the immediate crisis would be law enforcement's responsibility. Sheriffs and chiefs of police are shocked that OMB would propose that FEMA should assume responsibility in these areas where there is neither experience nor the legal authority for them to even act.

Perhaps more confusing is the contradiction of the January 2001 United States Government Interagency Domestic Terrorism Concept of Operations Plan, known as the CONPLAN, which states that crisis management is predominantly a law enforcement function, and includes measures to identify, acquire, and plan the use of resources needed to anticipate and/or resolve a threat or act of terrorism.

In a terrorist incident, a crisis management response may include traditional law enforcement missions, such as intelligence, surveillance, tactical operations, negotiations, forensics, investigations, as well as technical support missions such as agent identification, search, render safe procedures, transfer and disposal, and limited decontamination. In addition to traditional law enforcement missions, crisis management also includes assurance of public health and safety.

The contradiction of the presidential decision directives: Presidential Decision Directives 39, 62 and 63 direct the Attorney General, not FEMA, to assume lead responsibility for the Federal Government. It is the United States Department of Justice, not FEMA, that serves as the central agency in a crisis. That is what our local laws now reflect and that is how our personnel have been trained.

The Nation's sheriffs and police have established operational agreements with ODP and the FBI at the Department of Justice, and we should not be asked to scrap all of our policies, plans, and all of our agreements so that we can work under authority of an agency that has no law enforcement role.

Disruption of the current programs threatens the public. Last year, the Senate increased funding for the ODP from $250 million to $650 million, and we are now engaged in the planning for the allocation of these funds to law enforcement. Just as we are launching these new programs, OMB would have us terminate the effort and move everything over to FEMA. The disruption that such a shift would cause is nothing less than catastrophic at a time when the safety of the American people is at risk.

As elected sheriffs sworn to protect the public, we cannot support a recommendation that may cause enormous disruption and a potential interruption during this period of unprecedented threats to public safety in America. The Department of Justice should be commended. The National Sheriffs' Association believes that the Congress should commend the Attorney General, the FBI, and the ODP for a job well done, and not consider the transfer of their duties to agencies that lack the experience, training, and authority to get the job done.

As directed by Congress, the Department of Justice has worked with all 50 States on preparedness plans, and I am advised that 44 have been received. Relying upon decades of experience with review and approval of such State plans, ODP has already approved 40 of these State strategy documents.

I asked the Department of Justice to provide me with a listing of what they have done to assist law enforcement and first responders, and I am pleased to submit these figures for the record, which is part of the testimony.

Chairman BIDEN. Without objection, they will be submitted.

Sheriff FERRELL. At this time of national crisis, sheriffs want to support the efforts of the President and Governor Ridge. However, we cannot support the OMB recommendation to remove the Office of Domestic Preparedness from the United States Department of Justice and transfer this function to FEMA.

While this plan may appear to serve the interests of efficiency, it fails to recognize the reality of law enforcement responsibilities at the time of a terrorist attack. This sort of force consolidation can only lead to confusion, and that is not what our Nation needs right now.

Mr. Chairman, thank you for the opportunity to appear before you and I am prepared to answer the committee's questions at this time on this issue.

[The prepared statement of Sheriff Ferrell follows:]

TESTIMONY OF SHERIFF TOMMY FERRELL, FIRST VICE PRESIDENT, NATIONAL SHERIFFS' ASSOCIATION

INTRODUCTION

Mr. Chairman, I am Sheriff Tommy Ferrell from Adams County, Mississippi and I appear before you as First Vice President of the National Sheriffs' Association. I will take office as President in June.

The National Sheriffs' Association is surprised and deeply concerned about the proposal by OMB to eliminate the Office of Domestic Preparedness (ODP) at the U.S. Department of Justice, and to shift these responsibilities to the Federal Emergency Management Agency (FEMA).

This is a time when the American people need continuity and coordination, not the disruption of unnecessary reorganzation. For this reason, I appear before you today to add the voice of the Nation's Sheriffs to other law enforcement organizations that likewise oppose this OMB proposal. While we appreciate the efforts to OMB to consolidate functions and enhance efficiency, this proposal would unintentionally undermine the efforts of American law enforcement.

I will submit for the record a formal resolution adopted by the National Sheriffs' Association earlier this month, in which we set forth the reasons for our opposition to the proposed reorganization.

Let me explain each of the reasons for our opposition to the OMB proposal:

Experience With Counterterrorism: Sheriffs have worked with the Department of Justice on funding for anti-crime efforts since the Safe Streets Act of 1968. Over these 34 years, the Department of Justice has established expertise that cannot be replicated by an agency that is new to law enforcement. Nothing more need be said here, as it is apparent that there is no substitute for these 34 years of relationships and experience.

Contradiction of the Patriot Act: The Sheriffs of our Nation applaud your courage and leadership in passing the Patriot Act. But we are confused by the OMB proposal, since it seems to repeal sections of the Patriot Act even before some of those provisions have been implemented. For example, the OMB proposal seems to rewrite Sections 1005 and 1014, which direct the Attorney General, not FEMA, to make grants to Sheriffs for first responders, terrorism prevention and anti-terrorism training.

Law Enforcement Responds to a Deadly Threat, Not FEMA Agencies: Look at the record of terrorist attacks around the globe. Terrorists attack with automatic weapons, bombs, and often take hostages. Side-by-side with Federal law enforcement, we will face the terrorists, most probably with deadly weapons. We will never ask nor can we expect our Fire, EMS or Health personnel to face gunfire, explosives or other deadly assaults. That is the job of sheriffs and police, and it is ours alone. Once the threat has been addressed and public safety has been restored, only then it is possible to turn over the scene to the FEMA agencies. To do anything else would be contrary to a Sheriff's oath of office and contrary to the laws of the States. To subordinate our crisis response to FEMA would compromise the statutory obligation of law enforcement officials to protect their communities. Mr. Chairman, the House Subcommittee on Crime said it best in recognizing that this is the realty of both policy and practices across the Nation. They said that, "The Committee is concerned that FEMA is not the appropriate agency for these responsibilities. A terrorist attack is a criminal event, not a natural disaster." [1]

FEMA Role is Limited to Consequences Management: The prevention, detection and apprehension of terrorists are law enforcement functions, and it is not appropriate for training and coordination to be assigned to the FEMA regime, where there are no such responsibilities. If there were to be another terrorist attack, responding to the immediate crisis would be a law enforcement responsibility. Sheriffs and Chiefs of Police are shocked that OMB would propose that FEMA should assume responsibility in these areas, where there is neither experience nor legal authority to act. Perhaps most confusing is the contradiction of the January 2001 United States Government Interagency Domestic Terrorism Concept of Operations Plan, known as the CONPLAN, which states: "Crisis management is predominantly a law enforcement function and includes measures to identify, acquire, and plan the use of resources needed to anticipate, prevent, and/or resolve a threat or act of terrorism. In a terrorist incident, a crisis management response may include traditional law enforcement missions, such as intelligence, surveillance, tactical operations, negotiations, forensics, and investigations, as well as technical support missions, such as agent identification, search, render safe procedures, transfer and disposal, and limited decontamination. In addition to the traditional law enforcement missions, crisis management also includes assurance of public health and safety." [2]

Contradiction of Presidential Decision Directives: Presidential Decision Directives 39, 62 and 63 direct the Attorney General, not FEMA, to assume lead responsibility for the Federal Government. It is the U.S. Department of Justice, and not FEMA, that serves as the central agency in a crisis. This is what our local laws now reflect and this is how our personnel have been trained. The Nation's Sheriffs and Police have established operational agreements with ODP and the FBI at the Department of Justice, and we should not be asked to scrap all of our policies, plans, and agreements so that we can work under the authority of an agency that has no law enforcement role.

Disruption of Current Programs Threatens the Public: Last year, the House increased the funding for the ODP from $250 Million to $650 Million, and we are now engaged in the planning for allocation of these funds to law enforcement. Just as we are launching these new programs, OMB would have us terminate the effort and move everything over to FEMA. The disruption that such a shift would cause is nothing less than catastrophic at a time when the safety of the American people is at risk. As elected Sheriffs sworn to protect the public, we cannot support a recommendation that may cause enormous disruption and a potential interruption during this period of unprecedented threats to public safety in America.

Department of Justice Should be Commended: The National Sheriffs' Association believes that Congress should commend the Attorney General, the FBI and ODP for a job well done, and not consider the transfer of their duties to agencies that lack the experience, training and authority to get the job done. As directed by Congress, the Department of Justice has worked with all 50 states on preparedness plans, and I am advised that 44 have been received. Relying upon decades of experience with review and approval of such State plans, ODP has already approved 40 of these State Strategy documents. I asked the Department of Justice to provide me with

---

[1] House Committee on the Judiciary, Subcommittee on Crime. "Amended Views and Estimates"

[2] January 2001 United States Government Interagency Domestic Terrorism Concept of Operations Plan

a listing of what they have done to assist law enforcement and first responders, and I am pleased to submit these figures for the record.

Equipment

ODP has made $607.04 million dollars available to state and local jurisdictions for the procurement of specialized WMD equipment. ODP developed a Pre-positioned Equipment Program (PEP) to strategically locate emergency response equipment around the nation for response to terrorist incidents.

Training

From FY97 through FY01, ODP has trained over 96,600 state and local emergency responders from more than 1,548 different jurisdictions.

A total of 33 training courses are offered through ODP including a range of specialized courses, from basic awareness to discipline-specific advanced level training and directed toward a variety of disciplines including fire, hazardous materials, law enforcement, emergency medical services, public health, emergency management, and public works.

At its Center for Domestic Preparedness (CDP) in Anniston, Alabama, ODP operates the nation's only state and local live agent training facility, where emergency responders can test their skills in a live contaminated environment.

Working in partnership with the Combating Terrorism Technology Support Office/Technical Support Working Group and the FEMA Emergency Education Network (EENET), ODP provides regular awareness level training to the emergency response community through two satellite broadcast programs: Consequence Management News, Equipment and Training (CoMNET) and Live Response.

Exercises

In May 2000, ODP National Exercise Program conducted the Top Officials (TOPOFF) exercise, the largest Federal, state and local full-scale exercise that simulated chemical, biological and radiological attacks around the country. ODP has begun planning for the Congressional mandated TOPOFF II Full-Scale exercise, to be conducted in the spring of 2003.

A total of 93 exercises have been conducted by ODP to date. It is estimated that ODP will complete 220 exercises in FY02; including the NLDDP Program Exercises.

Working with the Department of Energy, ODP has established a Center for Exercise Excellence at the Nevada Test Site (NTS), creating a national WMD exercise-training program, which assists state and local emergency response agencies with the planning and conduct of domestic preparedness exercises.

Technical assistance

ODP has reconstituted the Domestic Preparedness Help line, a non-emergency, toll-free, 1–800 number resource available for use by state and local emergency responders. The Help line provides general information on the characteristics and control of WMD materials, technical information on response equipment, mitigation techniques, ODP programs and services, and available Federal assets.

Partnering with the U.S. Army's Pine Bluff Arsenal, ODP offers mobile technical assistance teams that provide on-site assistance and training to ODP grantees with the calibration, operation and maintenance of WMD response equipment.

Nunn-Lugar-Domenici Domestic Preparedness Program

ODP is responsible for completing the Nunn-Lugar-Domenici Domestic Preparedness Program that was transferred from DoD, effective December 21, 2000. As of January 31, 2002, ODP has completed:

- 22 Biological Weapons Tabletop Exercises (BW TTX);
- 6 Chemical Weapons Full Scale Exercises (CWFSE);
- All NLDDP final 15 cities Initial Meetings;
- 13 of 15 Senior Officials Workshops for the remaining cities;
- 12 of 15 Program Implementation Meetings for NLD cities 106–120; and
- 36 training courses for 8 of the final 15 NLD cities.

CONCLUSION

At this time of national crisis, Sheriffs want to support the efforts of the President and Governor Ridge. However, we cannot support the OMB recommendation to remove the Office of Domestic Preparedness from the U.S. Department of Justice and transfer this function to FEMA. While this plan may appear to serve the interests of efficiency, it fails to recognize the reality of law enforcement responsibilities at the time of a terrorist attack. This sort of forced consolidation can only lead to confusion, and that is not what our Nation needs right now.

Mr. Chairman, thank you for the opportunity to appear before you and I am prepared to answer the Committee's questions on this issue.

Chairman BIDEN. Thank you very much, Sheriff, for a very thorough statement.

Last but not least, Mr. Muhlhausen, thank you very much for being here again. We look forward to your testimony.

STATEMENT OF DAVID B. MUHLHAUSEN, POLICY ANALYST, CENTER FOR DATA ANALYSIS, HERITAGE FOUNDATION, WASHINGTON, DC

Mr. MUHLHAUSEN. Thank you, Chairman Biden.

Mr. Chairman, my name is David Muhlhausen. I am a policy analyst at the Heritage Foundation, specializing in crime policy and program valuation. In beginning my testimony, I must stress that the views I express are entirely my own and should not be construed as representing any official position of the Heritage Foundation. With that understanding, I am honored to be asked by the Subcommittee on Crime and Drugs to testify today on the needs of local law enforcement for homeland defense.

The September 11 terrorist attacks at the World Trade Center and the Pentagon reshaped Federal priorities to efforts that strengthen the Government's ability to protect Americans from terrorism. To improve anti-terrorism programs, Congress has shifted dollars away from wasteful, unproven or demonstrably ineffective programs.

For fiscal year 2003, the Bush administration has proposed three major changes to current assistance to local law enforcement. First, the administration plans to eliminate COPS hiring grants. This proposal is a good idea. Even with the best of intentions, COPS has not been a successful program when its performance has been measured by rigorous standards of social science research.

The Heritage Foundation's Center for Data Analysis conducted an independent analysis of the effectiveness of the COPS program. After accounting for local law enforcement expenditures and other socio-economic factors on a yearly basis, the analysis found that COPS hiring and redeployment grants have no statistically significant effect on reducing violent crime rates.

The administration's second proposal intends to consolidate local law enforcement block grants and Byrne formula grants into a single $800 million initiative called the Justice Assistance Grants Program. The administration aims to implement the Justice Assistance Grants Program with a greater emphasis on measuring the performance of the program. The consolidation of duplicate programs and the plan to measure performance are also sound public policies.

A third proposal from the administration is a request for $3.5 billion for the Federal Emergency Management Agency to improve preparedness of first responders when terrorist attacks occur. Many members of the local law enforcement community are concerned that FEMA normally responds only after a destructive act has occurred.

Currently, FEMA is not an agency well-suited to provide Federal assistance to law enforcement to protect against terrorism. Funding for law enforcement needs to be proactive, as well as reactive.

Not only will law enforcement be called upon to respond to terrorist acts, but the police are also expected to uncover and stop terrorist plots.

For this reason, Congress has set aside a portion of the $3.5 billion in FEMA grants for funding to help local law enforcement acquire the necessary skills and tools to prevent and respond to terrorism. These grants should be administered by the Department of Justice.

Funding could be used to help local law enforcement and the Federal Government develop a reciprocal relationship to share intelligence on suspected terrorist activities. In addition, the funding could assist local law enforcement agencies to conduct threat assessments and implement strategies to safeguard vulnerable targets.

From a policy standpoint, the administration's position on COPS, LLEBG, and Byrne grants is found. However, using FEMA to administer what amounts to local law enforcement grants is not. Congress should seriously reconsider the administration's plan to administer anti-terrorism grants to law enforcement through FEMA. Given the Nation's continuing vulnerability to future terrorist attacks, the Federal Government has the responsibility to assist local law enforcement in their efforts to detect, prevent, and respond to terrorism. A far better policy would be for Congress to transfer a portion of the administration's FEMA funding request to the Department of Justice to assist local law enforcement in the prevention of terrorism.

Senator I have submitted a copy of my written testimony to the subcommittee. Thank you.

[The prepared statement of Mr. Muhlhausen follows:]

STATEMENT OF DAVID B. MUHLHAUSEN, POLICY ANALYST, CENTER FOR DATA ANALYSIS, THE HERITAGE FOUNDATION

Mr. Chairman, my name is David Muhlhausen. I am a policy analyst at the Heritage Foundation specializing in crime policy and program evaluation. In beginning my testimony I must emphasize that the views I express are entirely my own, and should not be construed as representing any official position of The Heritage Foundation. With that understanding, I am honored to be asked by the Subcommittee on Crime and Drugs, to testify today on assessing the needs of local law enforcement for homeland defense.

The September 11 terrorist attacks on the World Trade Center and the Pentagon reshaped federal priorities to efforts that strengthen the government's ability to protect Americans from terrorism. To improve anti-terrorism programs, the Administration and Congress first should shift dollars away from wasteful, unproven, or demonstrably ineffective programs.

Second, Congress should recognize many crime programs deal with problems or functions that lie within the expertise, the jurisdiction, and the constitutional responsibilities of state and local governments. Therefore, these problems should be addressed by state and local officials.

THE BUSH ADMINISTRATION BUDGET PROPOSAL

For fiscal year 2003, the Bush Administration has proposed three major changes to the federal government's funding for state and local law enforcement. First, the Administration plans to eliminate Community Oriented Policing Services (COPS) grants for the hiring of additional police officers. This proposed is a good idea. Even with the best of intentions, COPS has not been a successful program when its performance has been measured by rigorous standards of social science research. COPS was intended to reduce crime by putting 100,000 additional officers on America's streets. Research by The Heritage Foundation, U.S. Department of Justice, and the General Accounting Office have all found that COPS failed to come close to the

100,000 additional officer goal. Despite funding of $8 billion between fiscal years 1994 to 2000, a 2000 report titled National Evaluation of the COPS Program, by the DOJ, estimates that the number of officers that COPS placed on the streets would, at most, peak at around 57,000 by 2001.

The Heritage Foundation Center for Data Analysis conducted an independent analysis of the effectiveness of the COPS program in 2001. After accounting for state and local law enforcement expenditures and other socioeconomic factors on a yearly basis, the analysis found that COPS grants for the hiring of additional police officers as well as grants for redeployment—the Making Officer Redeployment Effective (MORE) grants—have no statistically significant effect on reducing the rates of violent crime.

The Administration's second proposal intends to consolidate Local Law Enforcement Block Grants (LLEBG) and Byrne formula grants into one $800 million program called the Justice Assistance Grants (JAG). In the past, these programs have duplicated each other. According to the Office of Management and Budget, there is virtually no evidence that these grants have been effective in reducing crime and they lack adequate measures of performance. The Administration aims to implement the JAG program with a greater emphasis on measuring performance. The consolidation of these duplicative grants and the plan to measure performance are also sound public policies.

A third proposal from the Administration is a request for $3.5 billion for the Federal Emergency Management Agency (FEMA) to improve the preparedness of state and local first responders (police, firemen, and other emergency personnel) to respond to terrorism. These grants would fund programs that make responses to terrorist acts of mass destruction more efficient and coordinated. The funds will be used to improve communication, training, and technology.

Many members of the law enforcement community are concerned that FEMA normally responds only after a destructive act has occurred. Currently, FEMA is not an agency well suited to provide federal assistance to law enforcement for protecting against terrorism. Funding for law enforcement needs to be proactive, as well as reactive. Not only will law enforcement be called upon to respond to terrorist acts, but the police are also expected to uncover and stop terrorist plots. As Sheriff John Cary Bittick, President of the National Sheriffs' Association, recently testified before the U.S. House of Representatives Committee on the Judiciary, Subcommittee on Crime, "We will never ask nor can we expect our Fire, EMS, or Health personnel to face gunfire, explosives, or other deadly assaults. That is the job of police and sheriffs, and it is ours alone."

This is a sound observation. It is the responsibility of law enforcement to detect, prevent, and respond to terrorism. For this reason, Congress should set aside a portion of the $3.5 billion in FEMA grants to help state and local law enforcement acquire the necessary skills and tools to prevent and respond to terrorism. The Department of Justice (DOJ) should administer these grants for multiple purposes. Funding could be used to help local law enforcement and the federal government develop a reciprocal relationship to share intelligence on suspected terrorist activities. Training to give local law enforcement the tools to identify and stop terrorist activities could be funded by the grants. In addition, the funding could assist local law enforcement conduct threat assessments and implement strategies to safeguard vulnerable targets.

In any case, to enhance the value of every dollar spent on behalf of the taxpayers, the Administration should continue to review and reduce funding for ineffective grant programs, and continue the consolidation of duplicative programs into single grant programs.

WHAT CONGRESS SHOULD DO

As a general policy, Congress should always end funding for unproductive programs and consolidate duplicative programs. When viewed from this policy standpoint, the Administration's position on COPS, LLEBG, and Byrne grants is sound. However, using FEMA to administer what amounts to law enforcement grants is not. Congress should seriously reconsider the Administration's plan to administer anti-terrorism grants to law enforcement through FEMA. Given the nation's continuing susceptibility to future terrorist attacks, the federal government has the responsibility to assist state and local law enforcement in their efforts to detect, prevent, and respond to terrorism. FEMA's traditionally reactive approach to disasters is not well suited for the needs of law enforcement in responding to prospective terrorist threats. A far better policy would be for Congress to transfer a portion of the Administration's FEMA funding request to DOJ. Congress should keep in mind during these budget deliberations the importance of reviewing and reorienting its priorities. Especially after pouring billions of dollars in unproven programs through the years.

The Heritage Foundation is a public policy, research, and educational organization operating under Section 501(C)(3). It is privately supported, and receives no funds from any government at any level, nor does it perform any government or other contract work.

The Heritage Foundation is the most broadly supported think tank in the United States. During 2001, it had more than 200,000 individual, foundation, and corporate supporters representing every state in the U.S. Its 2001 contributions came from the following sources:

	Percent
Individuals	60.93
Foundations	27.02
Corporations	7.61
Investment Income	1.60
Publication Sales and Other	2.84

The top five corporate givers provided The Heritage Foundation with less than 3.5% of its 2001 income. The Heritage Foundation's books are audited annually by the national accounting firm of Deloitte & Touche. A list of major donors is available from The Heritage Foundation upon request.

Members of The Heritage Foundation staff testify as individuals discussing their own independent research. The views expressed are their own, and do not reflect an institutional position for The Heritage Foundation or its board of trustees.

Chairman BIDEN. Well, thank you very much, David.

I failed to mention earlier that Senator Grassley, who very much wanted to be here, is a member of the Budget Committee. As you have been reading in the newspaper, there is one heck of a hullabaloo going on in the Budget Committee, trying to figure out how we put 10 pounds in a 5-pound bag here and what priorities we set.

I am almost positive he would rather be here right now than there, but he is on that committee and it looks like he is not going to be able to get away. They are actually marking up the budget resolution right now. That is Senate jargon for meaning they are deciding what they are going to submit to the United States Senate, to the floor. So I apologize, and particularly to you, David, since he asked very much that you be here as one of the witnesses.

There is going to be a vote starting fairly soon. I know that a couple of you have time constraints, so maybe I will ask you questions first, those whom I know have a time constraint. I am going to wait until about three minutes left in this—you know, we are like Pavlov's dogs; when those lights go on and those buzzers happen, we have to move. I will need about three minutes to get to the floor. That will finish the one vote. I will vote for the second one and come back. So the bottom line is I will be gone probably about 12 minutes.

For those of you whom I haven't had a chance to ask questions in the next 12 minutes could hang around a little bit—and I will understand if you can't because I have already trespassed on your time and some of you have come a long distance.

Chief, I know your presence is required by the mayor at six o'clock tonight back in Wilmington, so maybe I can begin with you. Without giving me any number—if you have a number, I would appreciate it, but has your requirement to have more cops on the street, if this is the case, increased since 9/11, since the terrorist attacks?

I mean, what happens when nationally the United States Government, through initially the Attorney General—now, it will be through Governor Ridge—says that we have information believing there may be a terrorist attack on the United States, without any specificity as to where it may be? What happens to your police department when those—and they have happened, I guess, three or four times since then—what happens?

Chief SZCZERBA. We are about to the highest heightened state of alert that we can be, and I don't think the city of Wilmington is any different from any other city, small or large, throughout the country.

Chairman BIDEN. You have a port, correct, that you have to deal with?

Chief SZCZERBA. That is correct. We have a port. We have, I believe, the sixth busiest Amtrak station in the country, which you are well familiar with. We have other vulnerable sites that we have to monitor since then. And it is not only in staffing, but it has caused us to now have cameras set up and monitoring some areas which we never monitored before.

Chairman BIDEN. Has that put additional strains on your budget when you go to the city council? I am not trying to lead you. I give you my word, I am trying to figure this out.

Do you need more money to do the same job now because you have increased responsibilities as a practical matter, or can you get by on the same amount of money you have had if you are just going to do the same job you did last year?

Chief SZCZERBA. We could not get by on the same amount because we are going to fall behind. We have to address the homeland security issues, but like I stated in my prepared remarks, we also have the terrorists that are on our street corners on a daily basis that we also have to deal with.

Chairman BIDEN. One last question for you, Chief. You have been on the force a while. And maybe you can't answer this. It may be an unfair question, but I am going to ask it to you anyway and if you don't want to answer it, you don't have to.

Do you have any indication from the city council or the mayor's office for the upcoming budget that you might have to trim your budget if there is not a continuation of the COPS program and the same amount of money for the block grants and the Byrne grants?

Maybe you can tell me about the budget prospects, as you see them. Assuming the President's budget goes through, what do you envision? What kind of budget are you going to have to submit to the mayor?

Chief SZCZERBA. A strained budget. Not releasing any information because the mayor will be making his budget address tonight, but we would be facing not cuts, but it is a cut in the sense that in this next fiscal year I had anticipated having an academy class. That may be frozen right now.

Chairman BIDEN. By academy class you mean continuing to add police to your department?

Chief SZCZERBA. That is correct, to keep us up to our authorized strength, which is 289.

Chairman BIDEN. Because you have retirees?

Chief SZCZERBA. Yes, and by my request we would be adding 7 to that 289. But I know that won't happen, so I have to strike a mid-ground here to where I can maintain what I have. And to face a freeze, I am afraid that we would be taking steps back to what I demonstrated we faced in 1996 and I do not want to see that happen.

Chairman BIDEN. Before you have to leave to catch the four o'clock train, I want to ask this question to everyone, as well. Are any of you opposing spending more money just in the aggregate to deal with helping first responders in terms of firefighters, ambulances and the like?

You are not arguing that they shouldn't get more help, are you? Can you speak to that? Do you think the fire department, for example, in the city of Wilmington needs more assistance?

Chief SZCZERBA. Yes, I do.

Chairman BIDEN. Gentlemen, do any of you want to speak to that? Mr. Muhlhausen?

Mr. MUHLHAUSEN. Chairman Biden, I think that, in general, to prepare for terrorist attacks and the consequences, there is a Federal role in this area for first responders. So I don't think it is a debate about cutting funding for first responders, but I think that law enforcement plays a unique role. Not only do they have to respond after something has occurred, but they are also called in to prevent things, to stop things from happening. So FEMA is not the agency that is well-suited for that.

Chairman BIDEN. I will ask the mayors because you have the difficult responsibility of both of those departments. Assuming it wasn't taken out of your police departments, I assume you would welcome money for the training of and the equipping of your fire departments, your ambulances, and the EMS teams that go in. Is that correct?

Mayor HAYS. Senator, because of the downturn in the economy, I know my budget is flat this year. I wasn't able to support any raises at this point for any of our municipal employees. As such, what I am having to do is when I have the $188,000 that is being taken away because of the housing authority grant, I am having to make those kinds of choices and reallocate forces. I am having to acquire equipment because of 9/11 that I didn't have to have. I am having to prioritize some of the directions that some of my officers are having to go.

I have got the largest arena in central Arkansas, and as such we are obviously concerned about the gathering of 18,000 people at one time. My city has a hydroelectric facility, and again we are concerned about any potential terrorist act on that.

The one word that I have been able to use at least at this point in terms of responding to those needs is overtime, and that has had a severe impact on my budget. I might add that when I took office in 1989, the police department's budget in North Little Rock was a little over $6 million. Right now, it is a little over $16 million, and that is a 175-percent increase.

We have been fighting crime for those 13 years and have made successes with the partnerships that we have had with Washington. We are about at the end of our rope when it comes to additional resources. The COPS program, the grants and the partnerships we have had with Washington help us go forward, but they are not going forward at the pace that we need to. We started with

24 sworn officers through the COPS program. Right now, 17 of those 24 are funded by the city.

Chairman BIDEN. You picked them up, in other words.

Mayor HAYS. We picked them up.

Chairman BIDEN. That is how the program was designed to work. The first three years, basically we would do it. The last two years, you have got to commit to keep them two years. Then after that, you all are in a position of whether you can keep them. You are entitled, under the deal made, to let them go and not lose additional help from the Federal Government, because that was the deal. You didn't have to keep them forever. We hoped you would.

Mayor Hood, what kind of strain is it going to place on you?

Mayor HOOD. Mr. Chairman, I think related to what just stated, last week I shared with you that the last thing I am going to do is take police officers off the street. It is very important, when we have made that commitment to our citizens, that we make a commitment when we took those grant dollars up front to sustain them over a period of time. That is my philosophy.

I work off of a public safety master plan and a multi-year cycle, and this year I have been able to, since 9/11, advance an additional $1.5 million for additional public safety personnel needs. I project that with my new budget which I introduced to the council this summer that there will be an additional $2.5 million need for public safety personnel. That is above and beyond what I would have normally advanced through my public safety master planning.

We are also responsible for and have a unit of our police personnel at our international airport. Of course, there are lots of fluctuations going on right now with the federalization of certain employees at certain checkpoints, and when the National Guard leaves how long they will or won't stay. So that is going to be an issue that comes up as well.

Chairman BIDEN. If they leave, is the airport physically within your jurisdiction?

Mayor HOOD. Yes, it is, but we have adequate personnel at this point in time.

Chairman BIDEN. I know you do. I just want to make sure I understand.

Mayor HOOD. We may need to add more there, although we are reimbursed for that through our aviation authority.

As far as some of the things that we have been doing since 9/11, if there is an additional need that arises in the community, certainly you can kick in mutual aid agreements. You work at full-shift configurations a lot of time or go to the overtime situation.

Chairman BIDEN. But what do you have to cut, Madam Mayor? I would like to think if I were a mayor—and I don't like to think about being a mayor; it is a real job, it is a tough job.

But all kidding aside, you have made the decision I hope I would make, which is the last thing I am going to cut is law enforcement.

Mayor HOOD. Right.

Chairman BIDEN. Are you raising taxes?

Mayor HOOD. No. I actually lowered taxes.

Chairman BIDEN. Well, what gives?

Mayor HOOD. Well, I am in the fortunate situation right now that I have additional tax revenues coming in because I have grown my city through annexation and through population increases.

Chairman BIDEN. I see.

Mayor HOOD. But at the same time, I haven't determined yet if there is anything that has to be cut back.

Chairman BIDEN. I see.

Mayor HOOD. I think what you do is you look for a new business model. You look for more partnerships with the private sector and the non-profit sector. That is a new way of doing business.

Chairman BIDEN. Well, can I ask you a question? You represent, representing the League here, how many thousand mayors and municipalities?

Mayor HOOD. There are about 135,000 members that we have in the National League of Cities.

Chairman BIDEN. Now, I know you can speak for——

Mayor HOOD. No, but many of them are in situations where they are going to have to make very difficult choices. And while I can't give you specific examples from city to city and mayor to mayor, I know that that is something that they have been concerned about, that they are going to have to make some of those tough choices.

Chairman BIDEN. From everything I have heard—and I am going to get in trouble, me being a Democrat and you being a Republican, but you have been a heck of a mayor. I am not being solicitous. Your reputation procedes you here, so I am not being solicitous.

If you had to guess, and maybe you don't want to, if these cuts are sustained and for the next three years we don't have any of this COPS money and we go from, on the COPS side of the equation, COPS and Byrne, et cetera—the Justice Department right now has disbursed roughly $3.5 billion to localities for law enforcement-related activities over the last year. But it is being cut to 2, so there is about a $1.5 billion cut. These are rough numbers.

Assuming that kind of cut is sustained for the next several years, would you envision there being the same number of local law enforcement officers represented by your constituency, meaning the League of Cities, or is it likely that that number will decrease?

Mayor HOOD. I think by just some of the examples I have shared in my testimony and from other conversations and discussions I have had with my colleagues that many of them feel that they would have to not only make some difficult decisions as far as other vital services having to be cut back, but also perhaps the situation, yes, of having to pull officers.

Chairman BIDEN. The truth of the matter is——

Mayor HOOD. And especially small cities.

Chairman BIDEN. Yes, and that is where the rubber hits the road.

You are not a small city, Pat, but you are not the size of Orlando. What is your population again?

Mayor HAYS. Sixty thousand, Senator.

Chairman BIDEN. Sixty thousand.

Mayor HAYS. Yes. What you would probably find me doing is I am not going to get in a position where I have to cut officers, and so I am going to do everything I can. Now, I may be in a situation where I have to look to take some of my school resource officers out of the campus. The city pays 100 percent of their salary and I may have to take some and reallocate them from some of the neighborhood programs that we have in terms of how we have dispensed our police department in four different areas in our city.

I am going to meet the need. I am not going to cut my police department, but I may have to reallocate it, and that will cause, in my opinion, long-term damage to the quality of life in my community.

Chairman BIDEN. I have about 60 seconds to get over there and vote. I do want to raise some questions of you, Sheriff, if I may, as well. And, Mr. Muhlhausen, I want to talk to you about this notion of devolution of government and the responsibility of the Federal Government, to the extent it exists, and where and why. And, Bill, I would like to ask you some questions about the additional responsibilities you have.

Again, I do not in any way question the good intentions of the administration in making this shift, but I do question the judgment. And I wonder if you all are willing to give me some insight, to the extent that you have divined it, as to why we are moving this way. I mean, what do we expect to have happen?

Chief, with all due respect, I would like you to leave because the mayor will be very upset with me if his chief is not there when he submits his budget. To walk to the train station it will take you about 11 minutes. You have 20. Not that I have any authority over you, but I would like you to go because the mayor is a close friend of mine and I don't want to get in trouble with the mayor. But I thank you for coming down here. Thank you very much.

Chief SZCZERBA. Thank you, Senator.

Chairman BIDEN. With your permission, if you are willing to wait about 12 minutes, I am going to recess the hearing, to be absolutely certain for 15 minutes. We will reconvene here at five minutes of four, and I promise I will not keep you very long after that, if you are willing to wait. Thank you all very much.

We will recess for 15 minutes.

[The subcommittee stood in recess from 3:40 p.m. to 4:14 p.m.]

Chairman BIDEN. We will come back to order. I apologize. There was more than one vote.

At any rate, I understand both of our mayors had to leave and I will submit several questions to them in writing.

I would ask unanimous consent that additional statements be put in the record. Senator Grassley's statement, Senator Kohl's, and the Police Executive Research Forum will be entered into the record at this time.

[The prepared statement of Senator Grassley follows:]

STATEMENT OF SENATOR CHARLES E. GRASSLEY, HOMELAND DEFENSE: ASSESSING LOCAL LAW ENFORCEMENT NEEDS

Mr. Chairman, thank you for holding this hearing on how the Administration's budget will address the needs of local law enforcement. This hearing is particularly timely in light of the homeland defense mission that local law enforcement is now faced with. Of course, local law enforcement has always been the first line of defense against any crime, and as September 11th demonstrated, they are also the first to rush into harms way.

Because of the increased focus on homeland security, I conducted two working meetings last November in Des Moines and Cedar Rapids. I met with Iowa first responders to discuss their preparedness for responding to terrorists incidents and to learn how the federal government could better meet first responder needs. In these meetings, the various police offices present told me that to be fully prepared to respond to a terrorist incident, they would have to have additional funds for technology, communications equipment, and training.

They also informed me that the complex network of agencies offering resources, each with duplicative training and funding missions, has created a great deal of confusion for those trying to obtain assistance. These law enforcement and other first responders asked that the federal government provide a streamlined and simple grant process, and that there be more flexibility in how they can spend law enforcement funding. To give them what they need, the various local law enforcement funding programs have to be adjusted. The President's budget purports to do this by merging funding programs that have duplicative functions, and cutting or eliminating those programs that are inefficient or ineffective.

We're here today to discuss what impact the proposed cuts and mergers in the President's budget will have on local law enforcement funding. As many of you may know, I'm a strong proponent of good government, regardless of party politics. As such, I generally favor combining grant programs that administer the same type of grants. In addition to ending duplicative funding, I also support the elimination of funding programs that have already accomplished their goals, or on the other hand, are so inefficient or ineffective that they will never accomplish their goals. I also support the transferring of grant administration responsibilities from one office or agency to another—but only when it makes sense to do so.

I look forward to hearing from today's witnesses. I'm glad to see that Mr. David Muhlhausen of the Heritage Foundation could be with us again today. Mr. Muhlhausen, who is no stranger to this Committee, has recently published a paper on the very topic that we are discussing today. It is also good to have Sheriff Tom Ferrell from Adams County, Mississippi, here with us. Sheriff Ferrell is the incoming President of the National Sheriffs' Association (NSA) and would like to testify about the NSA's concerns over the transferring of the Office of Domestic Preparedness from the Department of Justice to the Federal Emergency Management Agency.

I have heard similar concerns from other law enforcement organizations and also from law enforcement officers back in Iowa. Because of the many objections that I have heard regarding this transfer, I am eager to hear Sheriff Ferrell's testimony, as well as the testimony from the other fine witnesses.

Chairman Biden, thank you again for holding this hearing.

[The prepared statement of Senator Kohl follows:]

STATEMENT OF SENATOR HERB KOHL

Mr. Chairman, thank you for calling this hearing today on the COPS program. Since 1994, COPS has become an indispensable part of our ongoing fight against crime. When we ask law enforcement officers in Wisconsin how we can help them do their jobs and protect our communities, they consistently cite the COPS program as the most beneficial use of federal money. We have received countless requests for community police—from small towns with only two or three officers to the largest cities in Wisconsin. Police departments and sheriffs' offices throughout the state have benefitted from the 1,340 new officers in Wisconsin since the program began.

Some choose to spend their time debating whether the COPS program is responsible for the consistently decreasing crime rate. A recent study found that a one dollar increase in hiring grants per resident has led to a corresponding decline of 5.26 violent crimes and 21.63 property crimes per 100,000 people. The few opponents of the program quarrel with those statistics. While that is an interesting academic discussion, we know what the police and sheriffs in our communities tell us—that COPS has made a tremendous difference.

Unfortunately, trouble lies ahead. The program's authorization has ended an the Administration has chosen to eviscerate the program. Frankly, we just do not understand this decision. After all, there is widespread support for the program. Last month, the Attorney General of the United States testified before the Appropriations Committee that the COPS program is one of the most successful government programs he could recall. The program works. The police organizations want it. Our communities need it. It is irresponsible to end it.

Mr. Chairman, we need to think about what comes next. Of course we should reauthorize the program for 50,000 new officers as you have proposed and a majority of the Senate has supported. And we should insist that funds directed to local law enforcement be targeted to hire new community police officers and school resource officers and to improve technology.

We must realize that the COPS program is more important today than ever before. To maintain our successes in the fight against crime in a law enforcement environment teeming with momentous new challengers, the COPS program is essential. Federal officers are more focused on terrorist threats, leaving local law enforcement with enhanced responsibilities. More will be expected of state and local law enforcement, and we must continue to help them.

The safety of our communities depends upon it. Thank you.

Chairman BIDEN. Gentlemen, let me begin by getting at, if I may, from the perspective of all three of you, and starting with you, Bill, what do you think the $3.5 billion that the administration is proposing be under the jurisdiction of FEMA for homeland—what do you think that means?

I mean, as I read the initiative, it says that none of the funds can be used for personnel expenses, including new hiring or overtime costs. It says that none of the funds can be allocated directly to any local jurisdiction, and it says that the funds require a 25-percent match contribution by the States, whereas the $635 million that all of you have spoken to that exists under the Justice Department now for the same purposes goes to the first responders in the States, administered by the Justice Department, without a match.

I know none of you like this distribution, but try to be as frank with me about what you think they think this allocation is going to—I mean, how is this going to work, in your mind? You have stated your concerns. You must be concerned because of how you think it is going to function. Talk to me about that piece.

Mr. JOHNSON. Yes, sir, and specifically the impact of that functioning will be on America's police. I think that it is clear that the administration's proposal is not a transfer of the COPS program or a COPS-like program to FEMA. It is completely doing away with COPS and it is simply transferring money at the same time to FEMA.

As other speakers and as you have indicated, clearly FEMA has an important job to do, and first responders in the medical services and fire services have a very important job to do. But as one of the other speakers also indicated, when you call 911 you don't hope for a clean-up. You are not looking for someone to clean up and decontaminate something next week. You want someone who is willing to come in and do whatever is necessary, even at the cost of their own life sometimes, to solve the problem that is here right now in an emergency.

In addressing it more specifically, I think as you indicated, the proposals that are out there are not long on specifics, although they may be in terms of what the money cannot be used for. Things such as preparedness or making plans or generically improving technology or communications sound good, but in reality there is nothing that is going to force FEMA to either put new police on the street or to maintain the police that are already out there who have been hired and funded with the assistance of the Federal Government.

Chairman BIDEN. Let me talk about for a moment—and I want you all to respond to all of this, if you can, so we can have more of a conversation here. Under last year's budget, within the Justice Department, there was $651,494,000 made available through the Justice Department for what they used to categorize as counter-terrorism programs.

Let me read what some of those are: the Nunn-Lugar response program, integrated training and technical assistance, Fort McClellan; domestic preparedness consortium, equipment acquisition grant program; situational exercises; research and development; bomb technology equipment program; virtual medical campus; Dartmouth Institute; Oklahoma City National Memorial Institute; NYU Center for Catastrophic Preparedness and Response; pre-positioned equipment.

Now, that was issued through the Justice Department. Some of that went directly to police forces. Some of that training went directly to police forces and others went to firefighters. They are the kinds of things, when we talk about preparedness, to meet a terrorist act.

Let me back up. When Senator Nunn was here, he and I introduced legislation dealing with the circumstances, if any, under which posse comitatus could be waived and you could call in the United States Army.

For those who are listening, posse comitatus is a very good principle in law. It says that there is no national police force, so you can't have the Army or the Navy or the Marines making arrests. That is the job of law enforcement.

We realized as we started to focus on this six years ago that you had problems like the prospect of a nuclear weapon being pre-positioned for detonation, the problem of a biological or chemical weapon being employed. Right now, the only people in the world who are really equipped, and not even fully equipped to deal with this are the military. You all don't have the training, the sheriffs or the police, to do it.

So we were trying to figure out, while we train first responders, including law enforcement, to identify the problem and to deal with it, there may be circumstances in which we may have to bring in the nuclear boys from the United States military to deactivate a bomb that is sitting in a tunnel, you know, like the science fiction movies you see where it is counting down.

We worked out a deal where they could only use force in self-defense and they would do it in conjunction with the police going in, but they could come in; they could be called in. Now, that is different than what is obviously a fire. You have airplanes hitting buildings, called the World Trade Towers, and then coming down. Obviously, you have to call the fire service, and the police responded as well at the same time.

But I assume you guys are talking about in terms of your responsibilities those many terrorist possibilities that literally have nothing to do with a fire being started or an accident occurring, but people who are armed, people who have weapons, people who have bombs strapped to them, people who have sarin gas in their backpacks, et cetera.

So has anyone explained to you from the administration how you all would be in on this deal for the $3.5 billion? Have they indicated to you, Sheriff—have they said anything to you? Have you had any briefings?

Sheriff FERRELL. I spoke personally with Governor Ridge when he came to address our conference a few ago, and of course the topic continued on into the conference room. It was explained to me by Governor Ridge that it was the position of the administration that in their effort to try to draw us all under FEMA, it was their plan to have an existing program, if you will, that includes all of the services, not only the responders, but law enforcement, to have it all in one location, under one house or under one roof, so it could be administered by someone in charge of the consequence management, I call it.

You alluded there a second ago about guns and bombs and what not. We in law enforcement don't feel it is correct procedure to put our friends in the other response agencies in harm's way. We respond to problems with guns and bombs and dangers and life-threatening situations all over the United States in the police and sheriff's business probably 100,000 times a day. We don't want to see our brothers in the fire business or in EMS be subjected—that is not their training and that is not what they were designed to do.

You mentioned FEMA. FEMA does not have a traditional law enforcement role. Not only do they not have a law enforcement role, but there has been no effort from FEMA extended to law enforcement to this point in time.

Chairman BIDEN. I got a chance to speak to your guys and women as well, and they seemed pretty adamant about this. What kind of responses have you gotten from the administration to your—"pleas" may be the wrong word—your concerns? I mean, what do they tell you?

Sheriff FERRELL. Again, speaking from a personal benefit of meeting face to face with Governor Ridge, we have not had much communication with the administration on that level. The only thing we have heard is the plan that has come forward, the same thing that you have seen in the form of the budget, with no contact from FEMA and very little contact from the administration.

Now, the administration has attempted in our last conference a few weeks ago to break the ice and to at least make contact, to start a dialogue, and that was the statement made by the governor at our meeting then to try to have a dialogue so we can start somewhere with law enforcement and the administration. That has been our last contact.

Chairman BIDEN. I have been trying to figure out how to avoid a fight on this. I am not looking for a fight. What I am looking for is somebody from the administration to come up here and tell us—Governor Ridge, preferably, because he is the guy making the decision, apparently; he is the guy under whose umbrella this is going to fall—answer some specific questions for us, because maybe we can work this out.

All of us want to make sure that firefighters get additional help and get additional training. But even with the limitation on personnel, I have met with the firefighters and the firefighters are upset about this, not about the shift to FEMA, but what this means. What they say is, hey, look, because of the additional calls on our time as it relates to terrorism, we need more personnel, we need more people, we need more firefighters to help us in this effort.

It takes me back to you, Bill, and then I want to get to you, David, about this devolution issue. Since you represent so many big-city police forces, what has been your experience when money and plans are deposited at the State level with the governor? What has been your experience as to whether or not your needs, representing an awful lot of major cities—you are in L.A., right?

Mr. JOHNSON. Yes.

Chairman BIDEN. Are you in New York as well?

Mr. JOHNSON. All of New York City, Los Angeles, Chicago, Miami-Dade County, Florida, Boston, Providence.

Chairman BIDEN. So you have the biggest outfits in the country?

Mr. JOHNSON. Yes.

Chairman BIDEN. What has been your experience when whatever the program is that is designed to help law enforcement starts its distribution in the State capital?

Mr. JOHNSON. Clearly that the funds are diluted from the top down. Number one, just by the nature of government—and nothing against the governors or the State officials, but of necessity not as many dollars will reach the local level.

Number two, the monies that do reach the local level, because they are being directed from the state capital, will not be as effectively or efficiently applied simply because there is a lack of knowledge. In the mining business, you would say that the knowledge is at the face, at the coal face where the miners are actually working.

In the police business, it is the actual cop on the street or the firefighter riding the back of the truck who knows what is needed. Therefore, it is the local officials, it is the chiefs, it is the sheriffs, it is the union officials, it is the representatives of the actual workers who are doing it and the local mayors who know what is going on in the communities because that is where they live and that is who they serve.

Chairman BIDEN. Sheriff, what a lot of people around the country don't fully comprehend is that in some States the most powerful law enforcement entity in terms of influence in the State are the sheriffs. What has been your experience from that position? The Mississippi sheriffs are a pretty powerful political force, I mean, in a positive way, being able to make their views known.

If all this money, whether it is through FEMA or whomever, goes directly to the governor and then it is decided by the State legislature where it goes, how have you usually fared?

Sheriff FERRELL. I agree with what Bill just mentioned. Even from a local level of the sheriff's position, the money is diluted. When it reaches the State level, it is almost non-existent.

As you well know, or may not know—you mentioned the office of sheriff in the United States, and in a lot of places it is different. In my area of the country, it is a constitutionally-elected office, a very powerful office, and he is known as the chief law enforcement agent of his county. Because of that position, that puts him in direct competition not only politically with the State administration, but also professionally with, in my part of the country, most State police agencies, if they exist, or departments of public safety that are the pet children of the governor or the State government, and rightfully so. That is his area of responsibility. So because of that, when money is funneled down through the State level, that is where it goes.

I can speak for a large range of sheriffs throughout the United States, especially your Midwestern sheriffs, your West Coast sheriffs, almost all except along the East Coast area, and that occurs when the money goes to the government. One of the best things that ever occurred to law enforcement was when the direction or the funnel of money was arranged like it was through DOJ. It came directly to the law enforcement agency. That eliminated those problems there.

Chairman BIDEN. When we wrote the COPS bill, that is exactly why we did it that way.

Sheriff FERRELL. You had one chart that depicted a reduced rate. I could predict that that chart is very low in its estimate. It could probably take away as much as 50 to 75 percent, unless it is mandated by the Congress. Most of those monies would not make it to the local level.

I have to tell you a quick story, and I said I wasn't going to say this, but it occurred yesterday in preparation for this trip.

Chairman BIDEN. That is all right. Take your time.

Sheriff FERRELL. I had to make a quick trip to the rural county next door to me, one of the most rural counties in the State of Mississippi. The sheriff has two officers and himself to patrol the entire county. He has some cities that don't have a police department.

We had a quick lunch and I told him I was coming to Washington, and he said, well, I want you to tell those people in Washington one thing for me, Sheriff, that if they do away with the LLEBG or they do away with the Byrne formula or if they do away with any of the grants—one of those two officers in his county is a COPS-funded position, and that is the epitome of the entire program for rural America, when you see a sheriff that is pleading to not cut off his funding, or his law enforcement capability is ended. That just occurred yesterday, so I told him I would tell that story when I got to Washington.

Chairman BIDEN. By the way, that has been my experience. One of the criticisms of the Heritage Foundation is that it gets spread out all over, but I think it is one of its greatest strengths, quite frankly.

As you and I talked about before, a kid growing up in New Orleans is less likely to be introduced to methamphetamine today than a kid in that rural county in Mississippi you just talked about with a sheriff and a deputy or two deputies.

Sheriff FERRELL. Yes, sir.

Chairman BIDEN. The drug problem has moved to rural America because there is the least resistance there, because you guys in the big cities have done an increasingly better job. It is just like squeezing a balloon, a water balloon; you know, it goes out in other directions.

I would like to talk about devolution for a second. I think I understand the distinction here, David. The Heritage Foundation has been very straightforward and has been one of the leaders in trying to get us to change the paradigm in this city, and has been a very strong and articulate proponent of the devolution of government.

I know you know all this, but that is moving power and resources and responsibility—not always resources—moving responsibility to where it belongs. One of the strongest objections that I have had from the outset, and it is intellectually justifiable, is that the reason a lot of folks originally didn't vote for the COPS program, a lot of my Republicans friends didn't vote it, is not because they weren't concerned about fighting crime, but they thought that is a quintessentially local responsibility.

Therefore, for a lot of reasons, including civil liberties and civil rights, but also for just pure structural reasons, the Federal Government shouldn't be helping buy a badge at the local level, even though the Federal Government doesn't control that, other than saying it must be community policing.

Now, the Heritage Foundation and other think tanks with some very serious minds bouncing around in there have argued that in order to make Government more efficient and the way it is supposed to function, there should be fewer powers granted to and fewer responsibilities, in effect, taken by the Federal Government. Whoever is best suited to exercise the responsibility should exercise it, including paying for it.

I detected, and maybe I am making more out of this than I should, that that rationale does not apply to the $3.5 billion related to homeland defense, not related to who administers it. We agree on FEMA versus Justice, but you would be willing to let Justice administer the bulk of that.

What is the rationale of why that is not the same as the COPS program as it relates to devolution?

Mr. MUHLHAUSEN. I believe it boils down to the Federal Government has a responsibility to help localities face certain dangers, like weapons of mass destruction, certain things that are so dangerous to our way of life that the Federal Government can provide a role and help with providing technology, training, and those sorts of things.

Where the difference comes in with, say, funding officer salaries and paying for the traditional roles of local governments—I take the view of James Madison in Federalist No. 54 that protecting life, liberty and property are suited best to local governments.

Chairman BIDEN. Yes.

Mr. MUHLHAUSEN. I believe that we are increasingly moving toward more Federal role, more Federal interference. I am afraid that one day, for instance, if your bill, S. 924, becomes law, it is going to do away with the responsibility of agencies of permanently funding their own officers, and it wouldn't stop.

Chairman BIDEN. That is a legitimate concern.

Mr. MUHLHAUSEN. I am worried that one day every police officer in our country is going to be a Federal employee, and I think we need to be concerned about that.

Chairman BIDEN. Well, at a minimum, I assume you are worried that if they are not a Federal employee, they are being paid for by Federal dollars.

Mr. MUHLHAUSEN. Yes.

Chairman BIDEN. But the ultimate worry would be that they become a Federal employee.

Mr. MUHLHAUSEN. Yes.

Chairman BIDEN. Again, we have a philosophical disagreement, but I respect that view. I assume, then, that because dealing with terrorism, particularly foreign-based terrorist activity, is quintessentially a Federal responsibility—or to put it another way, no matter how good the State of Mississippi was, no matter how wonderful the State of Delaware was, no matter how competent the State of California is, it does not have the capability to, in fact, deal with terrorism by infiltrating organizations over in Afghanistan, Paris, Germany, or whatever. It doesn't have that reach, correct?

Mr. MUHLHAUSEN. I believe we are in common agreement on that.

Chairman BIDEN. Okay. I just wanted to make sure I understood it. I am not being critical of it. I disagree with it. Just so you know—and someday maybe we can have a cup of coffee—the reason why I think that local law enforcement, in fact, warrants the kind of Federal help I have been proposing and continue to propose is that no matter how well the State of Mississippi does its job, it can't deal with the drug problem. It can't secure the borders of the United States. It cannot set national drug policy. It cannot deal with immigration, migration and mitigation. About 60 percent of all the crime is directly related to that.

I am not asking for a debate now. I just want you to understand where I—I respect the view you have articulated. This is getting a little esoteric, isn't it, guys? And I know a guy from Brown and Georgetown has no trouble following all this.

Mr. JOHNSON. I am liking this, Senator. I am liking this.

Chairman BIDEN. The bottom line of all this is that I am worried about at this point, Sheriff—and I also say to NAPO and all the police organizations, the very practical problem that much of what you are going to be required to do in every sheriff's department, every law enforcement officer in the country, is aggravated by the increasingly looming threat of international terrorist activity, let alone domestic terrorists, as in Oklahoma City.

I don't want you to become like school teachers. We expect our school teachers to teach our kids to read, write, add, subtract, be good citizens, understand what home life is about, pray, and a whole range of other things when they come from families that have that primary responsibility and they don't exercise that responsibility.

I am a little worried here that while we are trying to train a sheriff, Sheriff, in your county on how to recognize and distinguish between cyanide put in a bus terminal or on a bus and sarin gas, or we are trying to teach you to be able to distinguish between what constitutes a smallpox attack versus a chicken pox outbreak, or while we are trying to teach you as first responders to understand and be able to determine the nature of the problem you are responding to, you have got to be trained to do that.

It is going to take a lot of time and a lot of money and a lot of effort, and we should be doing it, but who is going to be stopping the cat burglar? Who is going to be the guy and the woman out there dealing with the chop shops that are taking the stuff across Mississippi, into New Orleans, to have that new Mustang chopped up in 17 different pieces and made five times as valuable?

That is the concern I have, even if you were able to, through the $3.5 billion administered through homeland security, get the fair share and even if it was going to get down to your level.

Do you guys talk about it that way? I am not, again, trying to put words in your mouth, but I sit here and I think how do you do all that at once.

Mr. JOHNSON. Clearly, I think if we can imagine for a minute that the attacks on September 11 never happened, and it didn't happen and we were still sitting here today talking about the administration's proposed 2003 budget, we would still say it is a bad idea. With all due respect to the administration, it is a bad idea because we still need cops, both cops in terms of the individual man and woman on the street, and COPS, in the capital letters, the Department of Justice program that funds it. We would still need it.

The fact is September 11 did happen and we are at risk of something similar happening again, because America, like the cop on the street, is a target for bad guys around the world. America as a nation is hated for the same reason individual cops are hated in our country, because we stand up for what is right. We have got courage and we have helped out other peoples and other nations throughout history. Even when we were a new Nation, we did it and we were hated for it. So that threat is not going to go away.

We still need police, and we need the resources that only the Federal Government can provide for our entire Nation. The knowledge of how to apply the resources is at the local level, and the COPS program under the Department of Justice has already proven itself to be a great partnership for America and America's police.

Sheriff FERRELL. Crisis management versus consequence management. That is as simple as we can get. Even when there is a crisis that calls for assistance that you mentioned, Senator, continues on at a level that still affects us in our mission in a tremendous fashion. But it is going to be hard to convince those that are trying to promote this program through OMB that this is not the direction to go. It is like I like to say in a lot of my presentations, if it ain't broke, don't try to fix it. In this case, it ain't broke.

Chairman BIDEN. Well, let me conclude. I am going to, with your permission, submit only a couple of questions in writing rather than keep you here.

As will come as no surprise to Bill, and maybe not you, Sheriff, or you, David—I don't know—I have a really close relationship with firefighters. My State is one of those States, Sheriff—and it is going to sound strange coming from a Senator looking at Mississippi—we are one of the most rural States in America. Our largest city is 83,000 people. The next largest city is about 31,000 people, and then it falls off the cliff after that.

My State is one of those few States in America where we only have one paid fire department in the State. By the way, we are not the smallest State. We are the fifth smallest in population. We have a little over 800,000 people and one paid fire service. We have a totally professional fire service, all-volunteer, except for the city of Wilmington and parts of Dover.

In talking to the firefighters, they are wondering how this is all going to work, too, because if it all goes to the State level, in a State like mine how does it get where? Who gets trained?

In those rural communities which have fire departments that are totally professional, how do they get trained in this stuff, unless you conclude that terrorist acts aren't going to happen in rural communities, which I think is unlikely?

So I will make a prediction to you all that the one thing the entire panel agreed on is that FEMA shouldn't run the whole show here, and I predict to you that FEMA will not turn the whole show before this is over. It is my hope—and if anyone from the administration is here, I issue an invitation to the administration to come and explain to us and try to work this out with us, because no one that I know is trying to say we should not spend more money to deal with training police officers, ambulance drivers, EMS people generally, firefighters, et cetera, in the art of dealing with terrorist threats that they have yet to become accustomed to.

So I want to make it clear that the measure for me is if the net Federal commitment is increased, and by whatever name, whatever program we want to call it, we allow localities to be able to directly make a plea for their needs, including personnel, then they count me in on the deal. I am ready to figure out how to deal with it. But absent that, I am not.

So, Sheriff, you probably came the longest distance, so I appreciate your willingness to be here.

Sheriff FERRELL. Thank you.

Chairman BIDEN. And I appreciate, by the way, the sheriffs organization supporting my other legislation that we have to extend the COPS program. We didn't talk about that today and that wasn't the purpose today, but I can't tell you how much I appreciate it.

David, you are always welcome here. I mean it sincerely. It is presumptuous of me to say you are bright as heck. You make straightforward arguments, and I sincerely say you add to the debate and the discussion here. And your view is shared by many of my colleagues here, many of my colleagues. With that, I would like again to thank you all.

Tell old Scotto I don't have cuffs on my pants, okay? That is an inside joke.

Mr. JOHNSON. I understand, and I will give him the message.

Chairman BIDEN. The hearing is adjourned.

[Whereupon, at 4:50 p.m., the subcommittee was adjourned.]

[Submissions for the record follow.]

[Additional material is being retained in the committee files.]

SUBMISSIONS FOR THE RECORD

Statement of Senator Maria Cantwell

Crime Subcommittee Hearing on "Homeland Defense: Assessing the Needs of Local Law Enforcement"

Thank you, Mr. Chairman, for convening this very important hearing today. In the wake of September 11th, we have heard many people call upon local law enforcement to serve as our first line of defense for homeland security. Yet the President's fiscal year 2003 budget sends a very different message. The budget slashes federal funding for the COPS program by eighty percent. This program has been incredibly successful and has helped local communities put police officers on the streets and in schools. In addition, the budget merges the Local Law Enforcement Block Grant Program and the Byrne grant program, and cuts the funding for the two programs by over twenty percent.

Mr. Chairman, the funds provided through the block grant and the Byrne programs are essential to criminal justice programs in my state. These grants fund tribal law enforcement assistance, including a tribal court visited by Supreme Court Justices O'Connor and Breyer last summer. As the Justices noted repeatedly, tribal courts reduce the rates of juvenile repeat offenders by providing counseling by community members throughout sentencing. The Byrne grant is also the primary source of funding for the drug court program in my state, a program that has served as a model for much of the rest of the country, and that has come to be widely regarded as extremely effective in dealing with substance abusers. Time and again, local and state-sponsored initiatives made possible with federal assistance have become the national model for treatment of drug offenses. In my home state, drug courts have proven to be a more effective and less expensive alternative to incarceration. Drug court graduates are far less likely to be re-arrested than those who simply went to jail for their use of drugs. Drug treatment costs about $2,500 a year, or one-tenth the cost of incarceration.

More recently, Washington state has initiated several mental health court pilot programs. These unique programs are quickly proving to follow the same track as drug courts—serving as a cost-effective and sensible response to a unique portion of the criminal population and becoming a model for national replication.

These Byrne funds also help pay for the meth response teams that perform hazardous clean up of meth labs in my state. Washington currently has the second highest number of methamphetamine labs in the country, and the difficulty of fighting this drug, particularly in our rural communities cannot be overstated. In addition these grants fund our narcotics task force, the state public defenders, domestic violence legal advocacy and youth violence prevention programs.

As the witnesses today note in their testimony, these programs are successful in part because they go direct to the local community and allow local law enforcement the necessary flexibility to put these funds to the best possible use. Further these cuts come at a time when local governments are taking in less revenue and simply do not have the resources to fund valuable criminal justice programs and get more police officers on the street.

I am very pleased we have these witnesses here today to give us the real first hand local perspective on the value of these programs and the importance of maintaining consistent funding levels across these programs.

In just the last two weeks I have heard from Police Chiefs and local officials in Yakima, in Vancouver, in Bellingham and in Spokane, cities that cover the four corners of my state, and each group had the same thing to say. They said that these programs work, that they are effective, and that without federal funds they cannot be maintained.

In particular I heard from these officials about the success of the COPS program in their communities. Since its inception in 1994, COPS has proved that if we provide local law enforcement with the resources they deserve, crime will decrease. Since the passage of the 1994 Crime Bill, overall crime has decreased 22 percent. The COPS program has also played an integral role in dealing with one of the most alarming crime trends in our nation: school violence. Funding through the COPS program helps place school resource officers in the very places that our children spend a significant portion of their days. Not only do officers develop the trust of the student body in a way that allows them to be alert to potential problems before they occur, the program provides good role models and allows kids to put a human face on law enforcement. I had the opportunity to visit with two members of the Fraternal Order of Police last week who currently work as school resource officers in Yakima and Spokane, and both told me it is the best job each of them have had in their 20 years in law enforcement.

Despite COPS proven track record, the Administration has made clear by the release of its recent budget proposal they are not committed to this vital program. This is why I, along with over 50 of my colleagues, strongly support Senator Biden's bill to fund the COPS program and hire 50,000 new officers for our communities over the next five years. I look forward to voting on that bill in Committee when we return from the recess.

Thank you Mr. Chairman, for holding this hearing on the importance of federal grant funding to local law enforcement, and I look forward to working with you to ensure that our local communities continue to receive these valuable resources.

STATEMENT OF
FBI EXECUTIVE ASSISTANT DIRECTOR
ROBERT J. CHIARADIO
BEFORE THE SENATE COMMITTEE ON THE JUDICIARY
MARCH 21, 2002

Good morning Chairman Leahy. We appreciate the opportunity to be here to discuss the myriad of things we are doing in response to the issues properly identified by Inspector General Fine. We also appreciate this Committee's longstanding interest in our ongoing efforts to rebuild our antiquated information infrastructure.

We commend the Inspector General and his staff for a thorough, objective and independent examination of these issues. His report is instructive and his recommendations constructive. Because his findings go to the very heart of how we conduct one of our core functions, Director Mueller has had the report made available to all employees and has made it recommended reading for all FBI management and supervisory personnel. Its lessons will be part of our training and its relevance and importance will live far beyond today.

Last May, then Director Freeh outlined for Congress the massive nature of the OKBOMB investigation and the virtual flood of documents and information created during its course. He also expressed regret that our shortcomings pertaining to the records had overshadowed the enormity of the sacrifices and accomplishments of those Agents who successfully investigated this case. He candidly admitted that "we simply have too little management attention focused on what has become over time a monumental task ....the seemingly mundane tasks of proper records creation, maintenance, dissemination and retrieval have not received the appropriate level of senior management attention ... [and that] this episode demonstrated that the mundane must be done as well as the spectacular." He then outlined a number of steps that the Bureau had embarked upon to fix some of the shortcomings.

On Tuesday, Director Mueller stated that "Sound records management and document accountability are at the heart of the FBI's ability to support investigations and prosecutions with information integrity. There can be no doubt about the accuracy, completeness and proper disclosure of the records we compile during our investigations and used by prosecutors in support of prosecutions. The ability to maintain, access and retrieve documents is critical to our mission and equally critical to our ability to protect the rights of those charged with crimes. It also is fundamental to robust analytical and information sharing capacities, both functions that we are rapidly enhancing. In short, records management and integrity are core functions that demand the same level attention and accountability as any function we undertake. It must be a part of the Bureau's culture."

As Inspector General Fine outlined for you, there are a host of contributing factors. The methods we use to record and retrieve information are too complex. Our Automated Case System (ACS) was not very effective in identifying information or supporting the investigation. Our technology was inadequate. We lacked a true information management system and what we do have is not user friendly. Many of our employees lacked the training necessary to be fully engaged in an automated environment and a host of other issues as well.

But what we thought when this issue first surfaced and what we believe now has been confirmed by Mr. Fine. This is not a "computer glitch," although a more robust system would have helped. It is a management and cultural issue which must be forthrightly confronted. We can add technology, simplify our procedures and dramatically reduce the opportunities for human error. Doing those things are relatively simple.

What we must do and what we are doing is recognizing information management as the core function that it is. At senior levels, we must lead the Bureau back to where this function is accepted as second nature. We must put in place the structures and automation that fully support this core function and we must inculcate in every employee, ourselves included, that this new way of doing business is the only way acceptable. We must improve our records management practices, not simply automate what we've been doing for decades.

We are taking specific actions to address each concern raised by the Inspector General, and a number of significant steps are well underway to overhaul our Bureau-wide records management capabilities, to increase accountability for compliance with established records procedures, and to put in place the training and skill sets necessary to bring about full employee acceptance of a near paperless environment.

Borrowing a little from what my boss has said, namely that with the help of Congress, we have restructured to recognize that the creation, maintenance, use and dissemination of our records is a core function that must be fully supported by management as a priority.

We have created a Records Management Division to ensure executive direction and full-time oversight over all records policy and functions, consolidating all records operations to ensure consistency, thoroughness and accountability.

A professional records management expert, Mr. William Hooton, here with us today, has been hired from the private sector to run the division. He has been charged with modernizing our enterprise-wide records systems and developing comprehensive, enforceable policies and procedures to ensure records integrity. He also is charged with putting in place those quality control mechanisms that will detect anomalies and problems early on. It is critical that we manage information, not just the systems that support our records.

Congress has funded, and we are implementing, extensive agency-wide training aimed squarely at reforming our culture to one that exploits and incorporates technology in our everyday way of doing business. Director Mueller is personally providing the leadership for this.

We have retrained our employees on proper document production, maintenance and retrieval and the importance of records management as a core function. There will be continuous training over the course of an employee's career.

And, of course, basic to any modern system of records is a modern information technology system, and modernization of our information technology, as this Committee knows, is one of our top priorities. We are making sustained progress in this area. Congress has approved funding for the FBI to upgrade technologies and infrastructure for organizing, accessing, analyzing and sharing information throughout the FBI and beyond.

We are replacing the now antiquated Automated Case System in favor of a multimedia and near paperless "virtual case file" with significant improvements in capabilities that greatly reduce the possibility that future documents will be misfiled, lost or otherwise failed to be produced. The new system will dramatically decrease the potential for human error both by automatically doing many functions now done by manual intervention and by substantially reducing the number of opportunities for problems to occur that are inherent in our current systems.

This new case file document management system, designed with substantial input from street Agents, will be of benefit by greatly simplifying the records creation and maintenance processes, being user friendly, and by allowing us to manage "leads" far more effectively.

The FBI's computer network is being completely revitalized to provide a "data warehousing" collaborative environment instead of application "stove pipes." The creation of "data warehouses" and ample supporting networks provide easier and most robust access to and sharing of information and results in integrated databases. The need for ad hoc crisis software applications will be eliminated.

Private sector support will allow commercial software and professional scanning, indexing and storage of documents is being used to move us rapidly out of the paper environment that was so vexing in the OKBOMB situation.

All of these systemic changes and many others, including everything Mr. Fine recommended, are critical components to what must be a sustained, agency-wide effort. These fundamental things are as important to protecting rights as how we execute warrants and testify in court. The challenge is great, especially the challenge of changing a culture. We believe we are on the way.

Finally, although his exhaustive investigation found no evidence of any intentional effort to withhold information from defense counsel, the Inspector General's report also criticizes the actions of certain FBI personnel. We are reviewing these criticisms and will quickly move to take any appropriate disciplinary action. In the end, there must be accountability.

###

POLICE EXECUTIVE
RESEARCH FORUM

Written Statement by the Police Executive Research Forum Before the Senate Judiciary Committee

Subcommittee on Crime and Drugs

On "Homeland Defense: Assessing the Needs of Local Law Enforcement"

WE PROVIDE PROGRESS IN POLICING

Submitted by
Chief Edward Flynn
PERF Legislative Chairman,
Arlington County (VA) Police Department
For Thursday, March 21, 2002

1120 Connecticut Avenue, NW Suite 930 Washington, D.C. 20036
Tel: 202-466-7820 Fax: 202-466-7826 TTY: 202-466-2670 www.PoliceForum.org

Homeland Defense: Assessing the Needs of Local Law Enforcement

Police, more than ever before, are stretching their resources to the limit. They know they can't win the war against terrorism, but lose the fight against crime. They must succeed at both. Law enforcement professionals in this country need tremendous resources to carry out their mandate in preventing future incidents of terrorism and when acting as first-responders if the worst does happen—and still maintain the daily crime prevention and enforcement duties of the agency.

In a Police Executive Research Forum (PERF[1]) survey of more than 160 police chiefs soon after September 11, it was evident that law enforcement's greatest needs included improvements to local intelligence gathering and sharing, adequate equipment, more personnel, funding for overtime, technology and more.[2] Despite severely limited resources, police professionals have risen to the challenges presented by their additional antiterrorism duties, and know they can continue to make valuable contributions to the nation's efforts to prevent future incidents. However, they cannot assume these additional responsibilities without significant federal support. While the list of law enforcement needs included below cannot be detailed or exhaustive, the following should provide some insight into police executives' concerns. Given the broad scope of this hearing, this statement provides a general overview of PERF members' needs after September 11, identified in the survey and subsequent information gathering efforts, as they relate to federal funding and support.

PERF has long recognized the tremendous value of federal grant programs that help local law enforcement meet the demand for innovative and professional crime prevention and control. Attached is a list of examples PERF members have provided on how such programs as the Local Law Enforcement Block Grant, Byrne grants and COPS Office grants have resulted in successful efforts to provide better police services to communities across the country. These grant programs

---

[1] PERF is a nonprofit association whose general members are progressive police professionals dedicated to improving policing services through research, debate and national leadership. PERF general members collectively serve more than 50 percent of the nation's population.

[2] A copy of the survey findings is attached in the discussion draft on the local law enforcement role in domestic terrorism (October 2001) and is available online at www.PoliceForum.org.

now have unprecedented importance to local police.[3] With the new responsibilities in antiterrorism efforts, local police must learn to do much more with the already limited resources at hand. These programs have provided needed training and technical assistance, personnel, equipment, technology, innovative programs/approaches, and other support that is the lifeblood of police departments.

PERF members believe that these programs should be funded at the highest possible levels at this critical time to ensure that officers will be available and supported by the necessary equipment, training, and technology to do their jobs. We must remember that local law enforcement officers will be among the first-responders to any critical incident and will be on the front lines in collecting information critical to prevention and detection of terrorist acts. At the same time, communities will demand that violence, drug trafficking and other crimes not be ignored even in a time of heightened alert. Resources must be used efficiently and effectively to respond to all these needs. There will be an even greater need for progressive approaches and model programs that can be replicated across the nation to ensure that resources will be well deployed. Without adequate federal support, police will not be able to serve their communities and engage in antiterrorism efforts effectively.

---

[3] With COPS funding, PERF members have purchased critical technology to boost efficiency, implemented innovative problem-solving programs, and received valuable training and technical assistance, all of which have played an important role in advancing community policing across the country.

Byrne discretionary programs have included those dealing with juveniles charged as adults, hot spot enforcement efforts, multijurisdictional task forces on drugs, drug treatment programs, crime analysis mapping efforts and more. Other projects have included police working with coalitions to improve residents' quality of life, providing counseling and resources to victims and witnesses of hate crimes, police efforts to address elder abuse and exploitation and myriad other programs. The Byrne formula grant program has funded states and local units of government to improve the functioning of the criminal justice system, with a focus on violent crimes and serious offenders. Funds are used, for example, to support community mobilization, crime prevention education and local crime strategies developed by public/private partnerships. Neighborhood watch and community policing initiatives are also funded under this important program.

The Local Law Enforcement Block Grant program has been used to support crime prevention programs and for police hiring, overtime and other important resources. PERF members have been able to provide vitally important public safety improvements with this funding.

Current Federal Legislation

PERF members have long supported the expansion of electronic surveillance authority that keeps pace with new technology, and applaud congressional leaders who have worked to that end. Some of the additional federal funding directed toward antiterrorism efforts will also benefit local police. But while some inroads have been made into addressing the complex challenges law enforcement faces in preventing, detecting, and investigating acts of terrorism, it is only the beginning. Police in this country need ongoing support for community policing and intelligence gathering, for hiring additional officers and retaining those we have, overtime expenses, safety equipment and tools for officers, mechanisms for improved information sharing with federal agencies, advances in interoperability and the application of new technology, and more.

Supporting Community Policing and Improving Intelligence Gathering

Police chiefs routinely credit community-oriented policing with helping to reduce crime and improve police–community relations. We must not lose ground on either of these fronts. And because citizens feel more comfortable talking with local officers, departments have received invaluable information from citizens that will help them play a critical role in gathering information on suspected terrorists and preventing future incidents. Many have had critical knowledge about individuals living in their communities, largely from the information they have gleaned through community policing partnerships and improved citizen interactions. This local information is exactly the type of data federal law enforcement agencies are trying to gather now.

Community policing efforts have helped police prepare for their new expansive role in these challenging times, but there is much work ahead. It is important to remember that local police agencies have responsibility for working with citizens and local leaders to stabilize communities traumatized by terrorist attacks. Local police play a crucial role in reducing fear, as well as preventing and responding to hoaxes, hate crimes, and bomb threats. Citizen fear of additional attacks and unknown consequences will cause communities to look to local law enforcement for answers and reassurance about potential terrorist threats. And in the event of a terrorist attack, communities will place tremendous demands on local police agencies for information, services and other assistance. These agencies will have to meet the needs of citizens and other stakeholders, even while they respond to the scene of a terrorist attack and contend with more routine calls for service to address crime. These functions create immense strains on the agencies' officers and resources.

With funding largely from the Office of Community Oriented Policing Services (COPS), local police agencies have developed unique qualifications to assess these community concerns and fears that are critical to effective intelligence gathering. This is especially true in light of the emphasis on citizen engagement, partnerships, trust, information sharing, and collaborative problem solving. Through community policing efforts, local police are better situated to identify, assess and reduce threats to local targets. The momentum and capacity built on the work of the COPS Office must not be curtailed. Federal funding is critical to maintaining these partnerships, ensuring that adequate numbers of officers trained in problem solving methods are hired and retained, and that model programs and practices are developed and shared to guarantee that police agencies are using their resources to the utmost effectiveness.

Past success has been due, in large part, to the *direct funding of local police agencies*. The COPS Office has been dedicated to local law enforcement issues and has developed extensive experience and expertise in overseeing their efforts. That work and focus must continue to ensure that police can continue to have expedited grant application opportunities that are tailored to the unique needs of local police agencies. The quick deployment of grant funds that considers the way local police agencies operate has been critical to the success of many law enforcement efforts. We continue to need federal support that takes into account local police operations and needs.

Hiring and Retaining Officers

Even before September 11, police across the nation faced serious recruiting and retention problems. For example, according to news accounts, New York City reported that despite a $10 million recruiting campaign in 2000, just 15,000 individuals signed up to take the qualifying test—one-half the number who signed up just three years before. In Chicago just 2,200 signed up to take the entry exam in 2001, compared with 36,000 who signed up in 1991 and the LAPD has been operating about 1,000 officers below its authorized strength of about 10,000. Smaller agencies have also been experiencing the cop crunch. The situation has been exacerbated by the turnover and retirement since September. Local government budgets have been depleted by post 9-11 responses and other municipal expenses. Even finding matching funds to retain current officers has been a struggle in cities across the country.

In New York City, more than 1,700 officers left the 41,000-member force last year through retirement or resignation, *a third more than the year before*. The retirement rate is only expected to accelerate, especially in light of increased pensions that are based on overtime-fueled salaries since September 11.

Police across the nation have logged tremendous overtime in meeting the demands since September 11, in both crime fighting and antiterrorism efforts. Those costs cannot be maintained despite long-term demands for continued local law enforcement support.

PERF has recently begun conducting a research project on the "cop crunch" problem, but one thing is already evident from the preliminary PERF member survey results on this issue: Recruiting and retention are top problems in police agencies and federal support continues to be needed.

Information Sharing

Local police chiefs expressed concern with reciprocal intelligence and information sharing involving some federal agencies, even when locals provided information and other support to those very same federal agencies. Information exchange issues are complex, but must be remedied. The exchange of information between local agencies and the FBI, FAA, FEMA and others has sometimes been dependent on individual personalities and willingness to share. Clearly, issues of mutual trust and guidelines for protecting sensitive information continue to be an issue, though meetings with the FBI and others have resulted in a dialogue and level of cooperation that looks very promising. PERF looks forward to working with our federal partners to take on issues related to security clearances for police, the level of information shared, improving the quality of national databases and other concerns.

Information sharing, even among local jurisdictions, is hampered by lack of updated technology. For example, few states and jurisdictions have regional crime analysis and mapping capabilities. The handful of jurisdictions that do, such as Delaware's statewide Real-Time Crime Reporting System, require significant investments in hardware, software, training and personnel.[4] Without grant programs to support even basic crime-fighting efforts, police will be less able to respond to demands on its limited resources.

Equipment for Officer Safety and Technology

Local police agencies will need equipment and other resources for officer safety, technology for advanced intelligence gathering and analysis, and for communicating with other law enforcement agencies. The scope and type of equipment and technology goes well beyond the equipment routinely distributed to local agencies through federal disaster preparedness efforts. Police officers need adequate protective gear, self-contained breathing apparatuses and other equipment that will protect them as they respond to critical incidents. In one way, the country was fortunate that the terrorists essentially used conventional weapons. While hijacking planes and using them as flying bombs was a new form of terror, there were no biological or chemical weapons unleashed. Given the preparedness of many local law enforcement agencies, any officer responding to a biological or chemical attack would be like a canary in a coalmine—the first to experience the weapons' lethal effects.

No one is certain of the type of attack future terrorists may already be planning; and trying to map out all the different scenarios is a nearly impossible feat. The only certainty is that local law enforcement will still be responsible for responding first to any and all threats and attacks. After all, what is "homeland security" if it is not the local cops?

Officers need to be able to communicate immediately with their own agency and other first-responders to a scene. Local police agencies need new and additional equipment to enhance interoperability of wireless communications, as was aptly demonstrated at the Pentagon.

---

[4]LaVigne, Nancy G. and Julie Wartell, 2001. *Mapping Across Boundaries: Regional Crime Analysis*, Washington, DC: Police Executive Research Forum.

Arlington County incident commanders could not communicate with other responding agencies that did not have similar radio equipment. At the Pentagon scene, more than 10 local law enforcement agencies were on hand helping with the initial response, evacuating the area, securing the scene, setting up a staging area for emergency equipment, and engaging in other critical incident scene management. Communications were strained when cell phone lines were overloaded and agencies with different equipment than Arlington County arrived and were unable to communicate with officials already at the scene. Arlington County is fortunate that it and neighboring Fairfax County have mobile emergency response command centers that allowed the more than 20 police and fire departments on the scene to communicate. But without federal assistance, few departments can afford these $250,000 vehicles.

Local police also need assistance in coordinating with non-police agencies (e.g. fire, EMS, 911, FAA, health, hazmat, etc.). This will require much improved interoperability for communications systems and strategies for developing effective emergency operations centers. Local police will also need additional software to facilitate coordination. Further, a good model is required for how these types of large-scale critical incidents should be managed.

Federal support should be provided directly to agencies for training, technical assistance, technology and equipment. Most jurisdictions do not have the resources, technology and equipment that were available to local police serving the Pentagon and World Trade Center. And, those needs increase dramatically when non-conventional weapons are used.

Dual Use Technology

We have heard a great deal recently about the importance of dual use technologies, and also other innovative programs. Dual use is a key concept to keep in mind as we look throughout the government for technologies and programs that help police improve their information gathering and crime fighting capacities, and which stand ready to help police shift from these crime fighting roles to terrorism prevention or responses. Examples include radio interoperability, improved intelligence analytic capabilities, protective suits acquired for methamphetamine lab eradication, and so on. In fact, a significant percentage of the Byrne, COPS, and other grant-funded programs facing possible cuts would likely qualify as dual use. These programs should not be cut or consolidated at a time when police need a much better infrastructure to fight both crime and terrorism at the same time.

Summary

This hearing comes at a time of unprecedented demand for police services. While this written statement is not an exhaustive list of law enforcement needs, it should serve to highlight where some of the greatest local police executives' concerns are currently focused. It is abundantly clear that for local police to meet its expanded mandate to our citizens, there must be continued federal support for existing local law enforcement grant programs and additional resources for its new role in fighting domestic terrorism.

POLICE EXECUTIVE
RESEARCH FORUM

Chuck Wexler
Executive Director

October 2, 2001

Staff Contacts:
Gerard Murphy, Senior Research Associate 202.466.7820, ext. 317
Martha Plotkin, Director of Legislative Affairs 202.466.7820, ext. 332
David Edelson, Assistant Director of Communications 202.466.7820, ext. 321

Discussion Draft:

Local Law Enforcement's Role in Preventing and Responding to Terrorism

Introduction

The nation is embarking upon a new and vigorous fight against terrorism and local police agencies must be full partners in these efforts. While local law enforcement has always had a role in first response and critical incident management, they will be asked for the first time to assume new and uncertain responsibilities. They welcome this challenge, and believe they can make a valuable contribution to the nation's anti-terrorism efforts. However, they cannot assume these responsibilities without significant federal support.

The Police Executive Research Forum (PERF) is a national nonprofit organization of progressive police executives who collectively serve more than half the nation's population. PERF members have long supported the expansion of wiretap authority and other surveillance authority that keeps pace with new technology; we choose to focus, however, on local needs that may not be adequately emphasized in current federal proposals. Indeed, PERF members, such as PERF Legislative Chair Chief Ed Flynn of Arlington County, Va., whose officers were the first-responders to the Pentagon, have unique insight into the role that local police can play. The remainder of the paper presents the results of a preliminary survey of local police chiefs regarding their role, needs and recommendations for contributing to the fight against terrorism. Proposed responses include such measures as best practices in local police preparedness, model policies and protocols, and local and federal cooperation models that address existing intelligence sharing obstacles.

PERF Survey

PERF recently surveyed more than 250 police chiefs from large jurisdictions on their respective needs and capabilities in addressing domestic terrorism. PERF members were and will continue

1120 Connecticut Avenue, NW Suite 930 Washington, D.C. 20036
Tel: 202-466-7820 Fax: 202-466-7826 www.PoliceForum.org

to be agents of prevention and first-responders to acts of terrorism within the United States and PERF wanted to get a quick assessment of their needs to better prevent and respond to terrorist acts. Within 48 hours, more than 150 chiefs responded that their greatest needs were for funding; intelligence gathering and sharing; equipment and technology; and gaining access to information from federal agencies. They reported that they were most prepared to coordinate with neighboring police agencies; engage in critical incident management; coordinate with non-police agencies; and to develop written policies and plans for anti-terrorist efforts. Fifty-nine percent of the responding agencies have federal facilities in their jurisdictions, with 52 percent having commercial airports. Thirty-nine percent reported having a military installation in their jurisdiction.

The preliminary survey results have confirmed what we all suspected—that local police have a very significant role in responding critical incidents; stabilizing the community after an incident; sharing information with other police agencies; and establishing multi-agency task forces. The survey revealed for the first time that local police believe their role in fighting terrorism is expanding, and that they welcome this change. **In particular, they believe they can make a valuable contribution to preventing terrorism, by building on their community policing networks to exchange information with citizens and gather intelligence.**

Respondents indicated, however, that they needed more information and training on the nature, dynamics and operations of international terrorism and needed to be more prepared. Most responding agencies reported that they would rely on more general critical incident plans—with only 16 percent indicating they would rely on a terrorist incident plan. This also may reflect the absence of such specific plans. More than 75 percent of the respondents have no anti-terrorist unit. The remainder had either a formal, but part-time, antiterrorism function or a full-time unit.

More than 30 percent of the agencies reported participation in existing multijurisdictional anti-terrorist task forces involving local, state and federal agencies. The vast majority of responding agencies were aware of intelligence, equipment, training and technical assistance resources for terrorism preparedness. Far fewer were aware of model policies, programs or adequate financial assistance.

The areas in which responding police agencies said they wanted or needed additional training or assistance was—in order of greatest concern—intelligence gathering capabilities; acquiring and using equipment or technology; and accessing external funds. In the comment sections of the surveys, the overwhelming majority of respondents expressed concern that federal authorities do not adequately share intelligence information. PERF members proposed that local police support should include developing "best practices" model policies and protocols, technical assistance and training for increased preparedness.

Based on the preliminary survey results and discussions with many of PERF's members, the following outline and information were developed to help ensure that local law enforcement needs are appropriately and adequately addressed by policymakers.

A. Local police agencies have critical roles to play in preventing and responding to terrorism.

1. Prevention

- Federal law enforcement cannot do it alone.
- Local police can and will play a critical role in **gathering intelligence** on suspected terrorists and knowing what to do with that information. Many have critical information about individuals living in their communities.
- Local police agencies are uniquely qualified to assess **community concerns and fears** that are critical to effective intelligence gathering. This is especially true in light of the effects and progress of **community policing** and its emphasis on citizen engagement, partnerships, trust, information sharing, and collaborative problem solving.
- Local police can be used effectively to prevent terrorism if they **share and receive intelligence** information with other local, state and federal agencies, and are trusted to maintain the confidentiality of sensitive information.
- Police can and must play a critical role in other aspects of terrorist prevention, such as identifying, assessing and reducing threats to local targets.

2. Critical Incident Prevention, Preparations and Response

- Clearly, local police play a key role in preventing, preparing for and responding to terrorist attacks. They can provide important early warning systems and critical evacuation, emergency medical and security functions.
- Local police will have an increased role in developing and implementing **local critical incident plans** that consider many forms of terrorist attacks.
- Local police agencies will have to work with federal, state and county law enforcement and general government officials to plan and implement **coordinated critical incident management plans** that ensure the effective management of a terrorism scene.

3. Aftermath

- Local police agencies will have responsibility for working with communities and local leaders to **stabilize communities** traumatized by terrorist attacks. Local police play a crucial role in reducing fear, as well as preventing and responding to hate crimes and bomb threats.
- **Citizen fear** of additional attacks and unknown consequences will cause communities to look to local law enforcement for answers and reassurance about potential terrorist threats.
- In the event of a terrorist attack, communities will place inordinate demands on local police agencies for **information, services and other assistance**, and these agencies will have to meet the needs of citizens and other stakeholders, even while they respond to the scene of a terrorist attack.

B. Local police agencies need assistance in assuming these critical roles and implementing new relationships, policies and procedures.

1. Coordination Strategies

- There is a need to develop strategies for local police agencies to collaborate with surrounding law enforcement officials (local, state and federal) for preventing, preparing for and responding to terrorism. Local police must be equal partners in any collaborative efforts if those strategies are to be effective.
- Local police need assistance in coordinating with non-police agencies (e.g. fire, EMS, 911, FAA, health, hazmat, etc.). This will require much improved interoperability for communications systems and strategies for developing effective emergency operations centers.
- Local police agencies need to determine the nature of their role in the new U.S. Attorney-led task forces. Federal, state and local agencies need to develop protocols for improved sharing of intelligence and information to make these task forces effective. Local police chiefs expressed concern with getting intelligence and information from some federal agencies even when locals provided intelligence and other support to those federal agencies. (Some chiefs have proposed that local law enforcement executives may need to get adequate security clearances to facilitate information sharing when an incident arises.) Information exchange issues are complex, but must be remedied. The exchange of information between locals and the FBI, FAA, FEMA and others has been plagued by uneven responses that are largely dependent on individual personalities and willingness to share. Issues of mutual trust must be addressed and guidelines for protecting sensitive information must be established.
- Local law enforcement needs models for coordinating with other law enforcement agencies (e.g., federal agencies, other municipal/sheriff, transportation, state) that will allow for the exchange of intelligence (for example, the timely sharing of "watch list" suspects with identifying information on NCIC), crime analysis, emergency communications, and risk assessment information. Successful collaboration and information sharing programs exist and could serve as models for anti-terrorism task forces. Existing anti-terrorist task forces should be evaluated and integrated into any new federal initiatives.
- A federal office could coordinate the development of models and protocols either directly or through a contractor by compiling information and convening experts from around the nation to develop these models and protocols. Those sessions could include discussions and steps to alleviate obstacles to local-federal cooperation. A detailed survey could be used to identify "best practices" around the nation and this information could be fed to a task force comprised of local law enforcement leaders, as well as representatives from other law enforcement agencies (e.g., federal agencies) for distribution.
- A federal office could assist with the development of regional task forces (especially those involving just local agencies) by providing experts to assist in the needs assessments, project planning and training efforts. Existing anti-terrorist task forces, High Intensity Drug Trafficking Area (HIDTA) task forces, and regional crime analysis information systems provide many examples of effective collaboration. Any federal

initiative must build on the expertise and existing networks to reduce redundancy and provide the broadest foundation for information sharing.

2. Policies/Procedures

- Local police agencies will need assistance in developing sound written policies and plans related to investigations, intelligence gathering, and information analysis, as well as mutual aid agreements and memoranda of understanding with those agencies with which they plan to form task forces. This would include task forces with federal agencies but could also include regional task forces initiated on the local level and that involve primarily local police agencies.
- Local and federal agencies need to develop protocols that allocate the responsibilities and coordinate managing a critical incident scene (perimeter, search, rescue, recovery, etc.) with the need to initiate the immediate follow-up investigation. For example, at the Pentagon, local and federal agencies faced conflicting priorities about managing the scene. Local and federal agencies need to develop much better detailed protocols that facilitate intelligence exchanges while also maintaining the confidentiality of the information and sources.
- Following the processes outlined above, a federal office or its contractor could develop a report that outlines the essential components of regional task forces and describes content that could be customized to each agency.
- A federal office could assist with the development of local or state initiated task forces by providing technical assistance to agencies as they tailor the model policies/procedures to their own jurisdictional situation. The PERF survey revealed that more than 45 local agencies have initiated formal discussions to form anti-terrorist task forces.

3. Equipment and technology

- Local police agencies will need technology, equipment and computer resources for advanced intelligence gathering, analysis and sharing with other law enforcement agencies. This type of equipment and technology goes well beyond the equipment routinely distributed to local agencies through federal disaster preparedness efforts.
- Local police agencies need new and additional equipment, to enhance their ability to prepare for and respond to a critical incident. Interoperability of communications is a critical issue, as was aptly demonstrated at the Pentagon. Arlington County incident commanders could not communicate with other responding agencies that did not have similar radio equipment. Cellular communications are essential to an effective public safety response. However, peak use of cellular technologies caused communications networks to overload and fail, leaving public safety agencies without cellular communications.
- A federal office could disseminate funds directly to agencies for technology and equipment to enhance intelligence-gathering capabilities and to manage a disaster scene. Most jurisdictions do not have the resources, technology and equipment that were available to local police serving the Pentagon and World Trade Center. Those needs increase dramatically when non-conventional weapons are used.

4. Training: Local agencies need training and education in the following:

- Understanding the nature, dynamics and operations of international terrorist groups that may operate in/against the United States, and how that translates into more effective patrol and investigative functions.
- Understanding the locations, movements and plans of international terrorist cells that live, work and assimilate in local communities.
- Conducting inquiries and investigations into potential terrorists while safeguarding the constitutional rights of all people in the United States.
- Gathering and analyzing intelligence on potential terrorist activities.
- Conducting threat assessments.
- Managing critical incidents: Applying incident command protocols to managing critical incidents.
- Conducting post-incident investigations.
- Providing post-incident crisis debriefing and management for service providers and citizens.
- A federal office could coordinate the development of model curriculum for in-service and specialized training and coordinate train-the-trainer sessions.

5. Democratic Policing

- Police need assistance in dealing with the issue of racially biased policing that could manifest itself in new ways as a result of the recent terrorist attacks.
- A federal office could promote the dissemination/accessibility of all racially biased policing and hate crime resources, and coordinate the development of supplemental reports focusing on the issue particularly as it pertains to terrorism.
- A federal office could coordinate the development of the academy and in-service training and community education programs strongly recommended in the COPS-funded report on racially biased policing—tailored to include the new manifestation of bias following the terrorist attacks.

C. The COPS Office is well suited to help coordinate the efforts that will enable local law enforcement to assume and fulfill their roles. The COPS Office

- Has ongoing credible relationships and positive working history with local police agencies;
- Has an innovative and responsive grant making and training infrastructure that was developed specifically to meet the needs of local law enforcement;
- Has the oversight mechanisms in place to monitor local law enforcement;
- Has a history providing a timely response to local law enforcement;
- Knows how the strengths of local police agencies—particularly in this age of community policing—can best be applied to respond to this problem; and,
- Has the capacity to quickly convene law enforcement practitioners to focus on emerging issues.

POLICE EXECUTIVE
RESEARCH FORUM

Chuck Wexler
Executive Director

LLEBG, Byrne Grant, and COPS Funding: Working Paper on Examples of the Programs' Impact on PERF Members

The following are examples of how police agencies across the nation have successfully used funding from Local Law Enforcement Block Grants, Byrne Grants, and COPS Grants. While every grant recipient has a long story to tell, these brief summaries serve as examples of the importance of these programs and demonstrate the wide range of efforts they allow law enforcement to undertake to improve their communities. At a time when police resources and personnel are stretched to the limit, these grant programs help ensure that police will not lose ground in combating crime as they assume new responsibilities in fighting domestic terrorism.

Arlington (TX) Police Department
COPS grants have allowed the Arlington Police Department to hire 81 new police officers. These officers have remained part of the department and now comprise over 15 percent of all officers. The department has received $3.6 million in LLEBG funding over the last six years. This money has allowed the department to purchase new cars, radios, radar, and computers for use in patrol cars and headquarters. Byrne Grants have played a significant role in the department's involvement in a multi-agency regional narcotics task force.

Arlington County (VA) Police Department
The Arlington County Police Department received grants through the COPS MORE program for technology and redeployment. The department was able to replace outdated equipment that had been a major burden on officers' efficiency. The department was also able to use the funding to hire a crime-mapping specialist so officers could be assigned to areas of the community that most needed their presence. Through the COPS Hiring program, the department increased its force by 8 percent by hiring 28 new officers. This allowed the department to form the first of many highly successful Community-Based Problem-Oriented Policing Teams in Arlington. The department has also used LLEBG funding to replace broken and outdated mobile terminal units.

Bellevue (WA) Police Department
The Bellevue Police Department received COPS funding to hire four new officers. This was a crucial grant because the department was unable to fund new officers due to a very

March, 2002

1120 Connecticut Avenue, NW Suite 930 Washington, D.C. 20036
Tel: 202-466-7820 Fax: 202-466-7826 TTY: 202-466-2670 www.PoliceForum.org perf@policeforum.org

tight city budget. The department has used LLEBG funding to purchase laptop computers and video cameras for police cars as well as purchase a mobile command unit.

Boston (MA) Police Department
With COPS funding, the Boston Police Department developed the *95-96 Strategic Planning & Community Mobilization Project*, a citywide endeavor that brought more than 400 stakeholders (including sworn/civilian police department members, citizens, clergy, businesses and nonprofit organizations) together to craft individualized crime prevention plans for each of Boston's 11 neighborhoods. Each of the 11 teams met for more than a year to analyze local problems and create a tailored, community-based response. The project was important as a foundation for Boston's Neighborhood Policing approach.

COPS funding was also instrumental in the initial implementation of Operation Ceasefire, Boston's successful youth firearms use reduction program. While research and development phases of this approach were funded by other sources, COPS was the first funding agency to commit substantial implementation funding for police and partners. This approach to youth gang violence reduction was enormously successful, reducing Boston's youth homicide rate by more than 75 percent over the course of the funding.

Boulder (CO) Police Department
The Boulder (CO) Police Department has used COPS funding to improve efficiency through providing and enhancing computer equipment for patrol vehicles and data retrieval. COPS in Schools funding and Advancing Community Policing Grants have allowed officers to be dedicated to school needs including gangs, drug abuse, and violence while assessing the strengths and weaknesses of community policing programs.

LLEBG funds have been used for a variety of projects. These include technology upgrades to the bomb squad and forensics upgrades to investigate rape cases and accident investigation. Mobile computer systems have improved efficiency among line officers and dispatchers.

Byrne funding has been focused on helping the youth of Boulder. For example, the Keep Hope Alive Program focuses on improving academic achievement, reducing minority dropout, preventing youth crime and violence, strengthening family development, and improving parent employability.

Broken Arrow (OK) Police Department
As of 2001, the Broken Arrow Police Department had hired 17 officers under the COPS program, which enabled the department to reduce beat size, increase traffic enforcement, and add to the number of school resource officers assigned to the schools. Because of the increase in staffing, the department was able to implement an organizational structure that encourages community policing and provides time to follow through with problem-solving projects. In addition, the department has received two School-Based Partnership Grants that have cemented its relationships with the school system and the students who attend. Because the funding came directly to the agency from COPS, the monies were

not diluted by multiple processing and the application process was straightforward and uncomplicated.

Colorado Springs Police Department
The Colorado Springs Police Department has had several successful programs as the result of COPS grants. Success stories include the following:

In 1996, the Colorado Springs Police Department was awarded a grant to enhance community policing to combat domestic violence. Because of the award, a Domestic Violence Enhanced Response Team (DVERT) was supported. The DVERT unit collaborates with 27 local community-based and government agencies. The DVERT unit has produced multimedia training tools and provided on-site training and education to communities across the country. DVERT has been recognized as a national demonstration site for the Violence Against Women Office.

In 1999, Colorado Springs also received a School-Based Partnership Grant through COPS that allowed the department to hire a full-time crime analyst who works directly with the school resource officers (SROs). This position has been invaluable to the SROs. The analyst works with the SROs in gathering, processing and disseminating information that pertains to crime trends and criminal activity.

Colorado State Patrol
The Colorado State Patrol (CSP) used COPS MORE funding to purchase mobile data computing systems for 100 of its police vehicles. The program has had great success, from reducing response times to enhancing capabilities to apprehend suspects. COPS Technology grants have also allowed the CSP to purchase and install 71 cameras for its patrol vehicles.

Byrne Grants have allowed the CSP to fund a felony accident reconstruction team. Byrne funding has also been used to fund the training of officers to participate in the Desert SNOW program designed to combat drug trafficking in Colorado.

Fargo (ND) Police Department
The Fargo Police Department has received $1,821,406 in COPS funding since 1995. This has allowed the agency to hire 21 new officers and has enabled the department to deploy SROs, establish a community watch, a bike patrol, and assign individual officers to specific beats.

The department has also received $1,084,868 in LLEBG funding since 1996. This funding has allowed the department to establish a motorcycle unit, support gang suppression activities, purchase computer equipment, and create a Citizen Volunteer "Reserve" Program.

Gainesville (FL) Police Department
During the course of the LLEBG, Byrne and COPS programs, the Gainesville Police Department has been able to use a portion of its funds to assist a number of local

programs that include assistance to a drug court program for first-time drug felony offenders; creation of a female-oriented crime prevention program for first-time offenders; expansion of a counseling program for at-risk young men; involvement of young people in an organized Explorer Program; and acquisition of the Automated Fingerprint Identification System (AFIS) that allows immediate entry of fingerprints into the state database, bringing the department two years later to the number two-ranked department in the state regarding offenders identified through fingerprints. Additional uses of these funds included purchase of an automated mug photo identification system for photo line-ups; use of a video production unit for training, recruitment and investigations; development of a Compstat-type accountability/management system; development of a patrol program that focuses on alcohol and youth problems; as well as hiring 17 police officers.

Green Bay (WI) Police Department
The Green Bay Police Department has used COPS Grants to partially fund 14 community policing officers that specialize in problem solving and creating youth programs. Part I violent crime has been reduced 40 percent since 1995 with the help of this program. COPS funding has been directly related to recognition of the Green Bay Police Department by criminal justice academics and the National Crime Prevention Council for the department's problem solving efforts.

LLEBG funding has allowed the department to purchase investigative equipment as well as fund teen centers in partnership with the Boys and Girls Club.

Kansas City (MO) Police Department
The Kansas City Police Department has used COPS grants for a variety of purposes. These include school-based partnerships that focused on the community's middle schools, hiring civilian support staff to redeploy officers to the streets, and improved information technology systems. COPS funding has also been used to educate at-risk members of the public about methamphetamines as well as to develop mechanisms to collect and analyze racial profiling data.

LLEBG funding has been used to purchase and upgrade much needed equipment and information technology systems. The department uses Byrne Grants to support the Kansas City Interdiction Task Force that specializes in combating illegal drug movement and organized narcotics enterprises.

Las Vegas (NV) Police Department
The Las Vegas Police Department has used COPS funding to hire additional officers and put others back on the streets. COPS Technology grants have also purchased much needed laptop computers, modems, and mounts.

LLEBG funding has been used for a variety of programs and purchases. These include an emergency public service dispatch center, mobile data terminals, an air support helicopter, and a DNA typing system. Meanwhile, Byrne funding has been used to support multi-jurisdictional task forces on gangs and narcotics.

Lenexa (KS) Police Department
From this grant, the department hired additional officers and formed a Criminal Interdiction Team (CIT) that serviced the business area exclusively. The department contacted and recruited businesses to participate. Once a business signed on, officers trained their staff to spot criminal activity and formed a close working partnership with the CIT. This program prevented many crimes.

Part of what makes this a true success story is that the CIT expertise has been passed on to a new generation of officers. These officers have developed expertise in working frauds, forgeries and other crimes that have spread beyond the traditional retail section to all retail areas of Lenexa. Additional officers have also furthered our efforts to expand the Crime Free Multi-Housing project (creating a safe living environment in apartment buildings and areas) to the very large number of apartment complexes in the city.

It is safe to say that in this day of doing more with less, these very successful initiatives would not be possible without the assistance of the COPS Office and the positions it has funded.

Lowell (MA) Police Department
Department of Justice/COPS funding enabled the Lowell Police Department to experiment with the latest problem-solving methods that led to increases in safety and public confidence. Prior to the infusion of money from the COPS program, the department was seriously underfunded and understaffed, severely hampering its ability to respond to citizens and to maintain safety and order. The business community was so concerned they explored the costs of hiring private security. Real estate prices for commercial and residential property across the city had bottomed out. The COPS funds contributed to the addition of nearly 100 officers in five years. These officers are better equipped and trained with the help of COPS funding. The new officers are responsive to community needs and concerns while being aggressive crime fighters. The officers and citizens working together have realized a 60 percent drop in crime over six years and revitalized the downtown area spurring business, tourism, culture and sports venues. None of these changes could have been considered had the city not become a safer place. These reforms were made possible with funding from the COPS office.

Macon (GA) Police Department
The Macon Police Department has received COPS Technology grants that has allowed it to purchase 19 cameras and 241 radios for its vehicles. The department's LLEBG funding has been used to strengthen security systems and purchase records management software. The grants have also been used to fund a multi-jurisdictional gang task force.

Miami (FL) Police Department
The Miami Police Department has received $18,593,642 since its first LLEBG award in 1996. The department used this funding to pay for overtime, new technology, technology upgrades, and new equipment. This wide variety of uses has allowed the department to acquire digital portable radios, laptops, tools for Marine Patrol Units, as well as many

other important resources. Current LLEBG funding is being used to improve radio communications and purchase a bomb response vehicle for the Special Investigations Section.

COPS funding allowed the department to hire 422 officers through a variety of programs. These officers were assigned to community policing duties and programs that were designed by examining the strengths and weaknesses of similar programs across the country. The department has also benefited from COPS grants that hired crime analysts and upgraded critical technology.

Minneapolis (MN) Police Department
The 81 police officers hired in Minneapolis under this program were the catalyst for a nationally recognized community-oriented policing effort, and have helped reduce crime over 34 percent in 4 years, taking Minneapolis to the lowest level of reported serious crime since 1966. This significant reduction in crime would never have occurred had it not been for the resources offered through the COPS Office. The COPS Office provided the personnel, technical assistance and equipment that allowed the department to place significant resources into crime prevention initiatives that directly correlated with this drop in crime.

Modesto (CA) Police Department
The Modesto Police department has received $3.8 million from COPS grants. This funding was used to hire 31 sworn officers, purchase mobile computers and upgrade its aging technology. The department has also received $1.2 million in LLEBG funding. This has allowed the department to purchase a records management system and communications equipment. Finally, Byrne Grants have allowed the department to participate in a multi-agency task force that targets drug manufacturers, traffickers, and sellers.

Newport (RI) Police Department
The Newport Police Department serves 29,000 residents with 81 sworn officers. The department uses LLEBG funding to purchase communications equipment, computer hardware, and to support a new alternative sentencing program for juveniles. The department has also received Byrne funding that it has used to pay a portion of the new $100,000 computer system that the department is purchasing.

Redmond (WA) Police Department
In January 1997, the Redmond (WA) Police Department implemented a program to target the incidents of domestic violence with funding from a COPS grant to hire a police officer and a legal advocate. The Redmond Domestic Violence Unit also partnered with the local social service agency to provide more immediate victim advocacy. In 1998, the department received an additional COPS grant that was used to enhance the Domestic Violence Unit. The unit expanded to include an additional officer and broadened the scope of the program and its reach. The department has had a Family Violence Unit (name changed also) that provides expedient follow-up to all cases involving spousal abuse, child abuse and status offenses—like "running away"—that occur primarily in the

home. The Redmond Police Department seeks to proactively reduce the amount of violence and address the issues that lead to violence by promptly prosecuting those cases that are criminal and by providing legal advocacy services and resources to victims by networking with the many agencies who can assist in this commitment. The agency's 3-person team has delivered quality service by participating in a number of partnerships with outside agencies and by providing training. From January 1997 through March 2000, the Family Violence Unit received and reviewed 1,184 cases; they followed up on 999 of them; and 1,328 victims have been contacted to ensure coordination of services and needs.

COPS funding to get this unit started has had a significant and positive impact on this community to curb the violence that is occurring within the homes of many of the community members.

San Diego (CA) Police Department
Federal grants to the San Diego Police Department have allowed it to dramatically increase its automation. COPS MORE funding has allowed the department to come very close to its goal of having a mobile computer terminal in every patrol car linked to a new, comprehensive records management system. The department estimates that these advances save thousands of hours of officer time each year that can be spent on community policing or problem solving.

LLEBG funding has been used to purchase safety equipment as well as advanced forensic equipment. The department considers LLEBG to be important because its flexibility allows the department to identify urgent needs within the community and direct the funding accordingly.

Byrne Grants have been used by the SDPD to develop community alliances and specialized services to victims of hate crimes. The department expanded community problem solving by sharing crime-mapping access with community-based organizations. This cooperation led to the development of a single point of contact and computer network among domestic violence service providers throughout San Diego so that services are readily located and coordinated in emergency situations.

Santa Cruz (CA) Sheriff's Office
The Santa Cruz Sheriff's Office has received COPS funding that has allowed it to begin a school resource officer program by hiring three new deputies. Byrne Grants give the sheriff's office $250,000 annually to fund two full-time deputies and one assistant district attorney who are assigned to marijuana suppression efforts.

South Pasadena (CA) Police Department
The COPS money that was received for South Pasedena has helped to support efforts that were not fully realized under a smaller budget, and have helped the department to make improvements and updates to achieve modern-day standards.

Springfield (IL) Police Department
The Springfield (IL) Police Department has hired 23 new officers using COPS funding. These officers have become school resource officers or patrol officers. Two civilians have also been hired through COPS MORE grants to put officers back on street duty while Problem-Solving Partnership Grants have been used to train officers in problem-solving.

The department has also used five LLEBG grants totaling $1,322,349 to hire three civilians, purchase specialty vehicles, crime scene processing equipment, information technology upgrades, and pay overtime expenses for special enforcement operations.

St. Louis County (MO) Police Department
COPS grants have allowed the St. Louis County Police Department to hire 68 police officers since their first grants in 1995. This includes 35 school resource officers and 12 Community Action Team officers that use problem solving strategies in the most criminally active areas of the county.

The department has received a total of $1,424,669 in LLEBG funding through six grants. They have used these funds to install laptop computers in patrol vehicles and purchase vehicles for a new Highway Safety Team that is charged with reducing traffic accidents on the county's highways.

The department received Byrne Grant funding under the Narcotics Control Assistance Program. This money was used to replace obsolete crime lab equipment, assign officers to the drug task force and hire forensic scientists.

Temple (TX) Police Department
The Temple Police Department has received $525,000 in COPS funding. This has allowed it to hire seven sworn officers and contributed to funding and staffing of police substations in critical areas. This presence has contributed to a significant decrease in criminal and narcotics activity. The department's LLEBG funding has funded video systems and recorders for police vehicles as well as upgrades to the police helicopter.

Waco (TX) Police Department
The Waco Police Department has used COPS funding to hire 22 new police officers. Some of these officers were hired to work directly with community leaders while others have specialized in domestic violence prevention and investigation. COPS funding also allowed officers to partner with victims services providers in the community to prevent and stop domestic violence. COPS Technology grants were used to purchase technology and equipment such as phone systems, computer hardware and software, and network systems.

The department has used LLEBG allocations to support purchases of mobile data terminals for police units. LLEBG funding has also supported upgrades to dispatch consoles in the emergency communications unit and purchase of radios for officers.

Funds have also been given to the police academy to purchase and improve training equipment.

Woonsocket (RI) Police Department
The Woonsocket Police Department is an example of a smaller department with 101 sworn officers. It has received $55,190 in LLEBG funding that was used to pay for the overtime costs of staffing police substations and has also bought needed equipment. The department has also received Byrne Grant funding to purchase the Justice Link Computer System and upgrade other computer systems. Without Byrne funding, the department would be forced to remove the computers from its patrol vehicles because the annual connection fee of $500 per vehicle would be too high. Other systems that may become inoperable without Byrne funding include a computerized fingerprinting machine that has very high annual costs.

*All summaries are based on written submissions by the police agencies to PERF.

PERF Staff Contacts:
Martha Plotkin, Legislative/Communications Director, (202) 466-7820
David Bright, Legislative/Research Specialist, (202) 466-7820

The Police Executive Research Forum
1120 Connecticut Avenue NW
Suite 930
Washington, DC 20036

O